WHAT'S "IN"
C H I C A G O

A GUIDE TO UNIQUE SHOPS
& ENTERTAINMENT

MARIFRAN CARLSON
ANNE TROMPETER

WITH ASSISTANCE FROM JULIE ANN JOHNSON

Academy
Chicago
Publishers

Copyright © 1986
Academy Chicago Publishers

Published in 1986 by
Academy Chicago Publishers
425 North Michigan Avenue
Chicago, Illinois 60611

Printed and bound in the U.S.A.

ISBN 0-89733-200-8

TABLE OF CONTENTS

Introduction 7

Shops 11

Merchandise Guide. 121

Index to Shops 137

Clubs 141

Potpourri 197

Entertainment Guide 202

Index to Clubs 207

TABLE OF CONTENTS

INTRODUCTION

After months of urban exploration, we realize more than ever what a wonderful town Chicago really is. The most unusual, exotic and interesting shops and entertainment spots in the US are found right here.

Whether you're a compulsive shopper (like us) and an inveterate club hopper (like us!) or just an occasional browser or dancer, you're in for some unusual treats.

Chicago has the best vintage clothing shops east of the Mississippi, and its specialty boutiques with charming and innovative clothing and jewelry for men, women and children are second to none. And you can spend very little or a bundle.

The city's night life, too, is exciting and immensely varied. Chicago is a center for blues, jazz and reggae, and ethnic night spots and dance clubs abound in full color. You'll be pleased to know that the vast majority of these are neither expensive nor pretentious.

With a few exceptions, we have not included downtown and Gold Coast shops since natives and visitors alike tend to know these. There are exciting shops and clubs in these areas of course, but our aim was to go beyond the best known streets and into the neighborhoods where some of Chicago's most imaginative entrepreneurs have established businesses.

HOW TO USE WHAT'S "IN" CHICAGO

This book is divided into SHOPS and CLUBS. All entries are listed alphabetically within geographical divisions.

We have defined the geographical divisions this way:

The Downtown area runs from the Lake to 800 west, and from The Chicago River to Roosevelt Road (1200 south).

Near North goes from the River to Armitage (2000 north) and west from the Lake to Damen (2000 west).

Mid North runs from Armitage to Irving Park Road (3800 north) and from the Lake to Damen (2000 west).

Far North runs from Irving Park Road to the city limits and west from the Lake to Damen (2000 west).

Northwest runs from Armitage to the city limits north, and west from Damen to the city limits west.

South Side runs from Roosevelt Road (1200 south) to (63rd Street), and from the Lake to Halsted (800 west).

Far South runs from 63rd Street to city limits south.

Southwest runs from Roosevelt Road south to the city limits and from Halsted to the city limits west.

Each section is followed by its own alphabetical index. SHOPS is followed by a Merchandise Guide of more than 100 selected items and lists of the stores that carry them. CLUBS is followed by an Entertainment Guide, listing night spots by the kind of entertainment you can find there. CLUBS is followed also by a POTPOURRI section which lists about 60 additional entertainment places, with addresses, phone numbers and a brief description of the type of entertainment they offer. The POTPOURRI places, which for one reason or another were not included in the main CLUB section, are listed in the Entertainment Guide, with the name followed by P. The authors did not visit them for the purposes of the book, but they feel readers should know about them.

Finally, please remember that this book is not intended to be comprehensive. It is a more or less selective guide to some interesting, unusual places around town. Changes take place all the time, too, so that possibly merchandise offered, or groups playing, when we go to press may not be the same by the time you use the book. We have tried to choose shops and clubs that have an apparent long life-line too, but things happen. So be forebearing, let us know if we've missed something important, and above all, enjoy yourselves!

Marifran Carlson
Anne Trompeter
March, 1986

ACCENT CHICAGO

233 S Wacker / 60606   993-0499
(See listing under Near North)

BENETTON'S

25 E Washington / 60602   855-0775
(See listing under Near North)

CRATE & BARREL

101 N Wabash / 60602   372-0100
(See listing under Near North)

MODALISQUE

616 W Adams / 60606   559-0107
Hours: Tues–Sat 11:30 am–5:30 pm, Fri 12 pm–9 pm
concurrent only with gallery openings. Closed Sun, Mon
CC: Cash Or Check Only

Here quality vintage clothing and the latest fashions, some imported and some from Chicago designers, are displayed in the cozy setting of a Victorian parlor situated in the front of an enormous, impressive second floor loft. The stairs you climb to get there are scattered with silk nosegays. Owner Marguerite Horberg began the shop in 1985 partly to showcase little-known Chicago designers and partly to indulge her own interests in art and the culture and artifacts of Asia where she has traveled widely. Her shop in this uncharted West Loop loft area has the most unusual displays of fashions and jewelry we've seen. On one set of shelves, for instance, women's '30s and '40s hats were displayed with beaded silk flowers and old copies of *Look* magazine. Also in the vintage vein were delicate '20s and '30s chiffon tea dresses, lace cocktail dresses from the '50s studded with rhinestones and pearls, and a very elegant '30s Chinese embroidered silk jacket with matching trousers ($150).

For men there is a breathtaking collection of silk tuxedos and fine old jackets in blends of wool, silk and linen. Marifran crossed the gender gap when she bought a wonderful yellow rayon Hawaiian shirt for $25.

Back to the women: for those who want something completely new, there were designer Monica Robbin's pull-on tunics, dresses and jumpsuits in solids and Victorian patterns and Morgan Puett's outfits in cotton, linen and rayon blends featured in *Vogue*. There is leather jewelry, with inserts of alligator and eelskin, and I saw an unusual pair of earrings made of scrap metal and put together to balance like a mobile ($14). There are cleverly designed children's clothes here too: Spax's unique jodhpur and jacket set at $95 caught our eye and so did colorful plastic raincoats with insets of little fish floating in a pocket at $75. *And* there are selected imports: beautifully embroidered Afghan dresses ($80) and an enticing pile of sweaters (around $40). While we were visiting, Marguerite bought some dresses and scarves from a woman who had just returned from Morocco. These were snapped up on the spot by browsing customers.

The shop itself has the charm of an art-strewn parlor. It was a unique shopping experience. –AT

SATURDAY'S CHILD

50 E Washington / 60601   *372-8697*
(See listing under Mid North)

13

A CAPRICCIO

47 E Oak / 60611   787-9824
Hours: Mon–Sat 10 am–6 pm, Closed Sun
CC: M, V

Don't miss this shop—remember it's tucked away on a lower level. The specialty here is highly styled activewear and leotards. There are printed sweat suits in unusual colors and striking patterns ($80 to $150), leg warmers in wool and cotton blends ($10 & $12). Linda, the manager, says that the most interesting activewear comes from California and from western Europe. It's interesting to see all the countries whose exports are sold here. If you see an exercise outfit in a magazine and can't find it anywhere, Linda will try and special order it for you. In addition to exercise clothes, this shop carries dancer's wear: there is a wide selection of ballet shoes in a range of sizes and colors, and elastic dance belts as well as leotards. A Capriccio also sells sportswear and cruisewear and a full line of bathing suits available year 'round. There are one-piece and two-piece suits that are not be found at department stores. –MC

ACCENT CHICAGO

Water Tower Place: 835 N Michigan / 60611
944-1354
Sears Tower: 233 S Wacker / 60606   993-0499
Hours: Daily 9 am–9 pm
CC: A, D, M, V

Everything you could ever ask for in the way of classy souvenirs and then some is to be found at

Accent Chicago's original Water Tower location, and at their new 1900-square foot store in Sears Tower. Books? Buttons? Tie Pins? Glassware? T-shirts? You'll find distinctive gifts in all price ranges—some serious, some funny—but all marked "Chicago." Besides clever novelties, like a box of fortune cookies stuffed with Chicago fortunes, Accent Chicago has the best collection of graphics representing—what else?—Chicago! -AT

ACCENTS STUDIO

611 N State / 60610   664-1311
Hours: Mon–Sat 12 pm–7 pm
CC: A

Young, hip and friendly, Chicago artists Colleen Montgomery and Linda Darabi have opened this little shop to sell original jewelry and accessories designed by their friends and acquaintances, at less than Michigan Avenue prices. The setting is charming: silver wallpaper patterned with moons and planets is set off by the fuschia ceiling and mouldings; wares are displayed in hanging plexiglass cases. There are accessories here by 40 different Chicago designers. There are earrings: hand-painted tropical fish and birds, ceramic fans, rhinestones, enamel, plexiglass geometrics, clusters of beads and fake fur, which Colleen calls "earrings you can pet." Linda makes delightful necklaces from 1920's French belt buckles, and brass goddess necklaces with matching earrings. Accents Studio also does inexpensive jewelry repair, and custom designs. You can find silk neckpieces ($15 to $20), belts and handbags here. So take a trip to this friendly, creative little world. -JJ

ART EFFECT

651 W Armitage / 60614   664-0997
Hours: Tues–Thurs 11 am–7 pm, Fri 11 am–6 pm, Sat
10 am–5:30 pm, Sun 12 pm–5 pm
Closed Mon
CC: A, M, V

Two talented and enthusiastic women—Carol Master and Esther Fishman—opened this shop in 1984 in order to make available reasonably priced contemporary fashions by individual artists. The shop, which was originally called Artwear, has a gallery feeling, with hardwood floors and imaginative and colorful garments displayed on unusual fixtures. Ninety percent of the clothing and the extensive jewelry collection is on consignment, and 50% of it has been done by Chicago designers. All of it is one-of-a-kind or limited lines.

You can buy a handpainted cotton or silk dress with expressive splashes of color by Ann Arbor artist Lisa Marra ($220), or Grace Jeffers' handprinted dresses ($220) and sweat shirts ($50). Or you can buy cotton separates by Elizabeth Young, another Chicagoan, in black, white and gray, starkly shaped and very dramatic with boldly colored skirts. If your size is not in stock, Elizabeth can make up a special order and they change from season to season, in a $60-$100 range.

Esther says that her more mature customers like the many different lines of handwoven separates in the shop because they are classic styles that can be worn season after season. The average price of an outfit is $200. Handmade sweaters for winter are available in sumptuous colors in wool, mohair and cotton at about $125. To wear under these creations, try a set of hand-painted panties and camisole ($36) and kicky socks ($8 to $13). And to top it off how about a handpainted silk or cotton scarf ($28 to $100) from any one of ten different artists?

The jewelry complements the clothing, and is available in a wide range at good prices. Vicky Schwager makes earrings from silver, brass, copper and niobium (brightly colored metal) in various shapes. There are Marcia Wegman's earrings and necklaces made from Japanese paper layered and colored ($2 to $50) and ceramic earrings by Pam Doswell in pastels ($20).

The owners of this comfortable boutique went to school together and then teamed up here after trying different careers: Carol taught art and was a freelance artist and Esther did social work. They promote their shop through fashion shows in the north suburbs and with minglings of artists and locals on the premises. Be sure to stop by, put yourself on the mailing list and pick up some art effects of your own. –AT

BANANA REPUBLIC

Water Tower Place: 835 N Michigan / 60611
642-7667
Hours: Mon–Sat 10 am–8 pm, Sun 12 pm–6 pm
CC: A, D, M, V

Don't be fooled by the palm frond decor, or the panther skin tissue paper; this fascinating shop—part of a chain which started as a catalogue operation in San Francisco—sells real goods, with no nonsense about them: natural fabrics, earth tones, gobs of pockets, extra stitching and good details. The clothes are roomy enough for an active life, and many are unisex.

The men's wardrobe includes a goatskin flight jacket ($275), tweedy pullovers ($49), bush jackets in blue denim and khaki ($36) outback shorts and pants ($36)—one pair has zippers that convert long pants to shorts—cotton riding raincoat with an oil and wax finish ($129), an artisan's night shirt ($36) and a leather bush vest ($159).

Most of these things come in women's sizes, and occasionally with variations: the women's tweedy pullover, for instance, has dolman sleeves. Clothing just for women includes dresses in blue, rose or khaki velvety cotton with long sleeves, an elasticized waist and a webbed cotton belt ($69), the cotton Serengeti Skirt in khaki, tan and sand with a wide waistband and buttons up one hip ($45), easy cotton skirts with elasticized waists ($19), and comfortable cotton and flannel shirts at reasonable prices.

For both men and women there are leather belts, walking shoes and boots and a small but select group of linen and leather bags. Not the least interesting is an Israeli paratrooper's briefcase ($25). Before you leave, check out the green Swedish army ties ($12) and the leather bandoliers ($24) which my salesman assured me was great for holding credit cards. -JJ

BATTAGLIA

724 N Wabash / 60611   787-3237
Hours: Mon–Fri 10 am–7 pm, Sat 10 am–5 pm, Closed Sun
CC: A, C, M, V

Here you can find fine Italian leather handbags, shoes and some clothing. Vincenzo Battaglia, the shop's owner, designs and imports all his merchandise himself. Twice a year he travels to Italy to work with small artisans in towns around Bologna, where, he says, the finest leather goods are produced. He can give his customers an idea of the colors that will be popular in the coming season because he attends designer fashion shows all over Europe. He has a handsome collection of soft leather bags in the $160 range. You can request a special color in shoes or handbags and Vincenzo's artisans will make it up and send it here for your approval. If you are not satisfied you are under no obligation to keep the item. If you wear a difficult-to-find shoe size, this system may be just what you are looking for. You can do the same thing with suits, another Battaglia specialty: I saw a beautiful suede suit here trimmed with python for around $600. Special orders involve a 4 to 6 week wait.

Because of its convenient location a few steps from Michigan Avenue, Battaglia has a prosperous clientele who know a stylish bargain when they see one: former Mayor Jane Byrne, CBS News commentator Susan Anderson and Channel 7's Oprah Winfrey are just a few of the local celebrities who share our addiction to fine leather goods. Some socialites bring their clothes into the shop so that Vincenzo or Gregg Fields, the manager, can help them find the right bag or pumps to complete their look. But Battaglia does not cater only to the rich and famous: Vincenzo specifically stays open until 7 pm on week nights so that he can accommodate women who work downtown. All the products are designed with the practical needs of the American woman in mind, although elegance is never sacrificed for practicality. Low-heeled shoes on sale here are beautiful as well as comfortable, and store policy requires that no customer leave the shop with shoes unless they are sure there is a perfect fit. So drop in and take a look. I can tell you that, I, myself, have never left this shop without a package. -MC

BEAUTY AND THE BEAST

Water Tower Place: 835 N Michigan / 60611
944-7570
Hours: Mon & Thurs 10 am-7 pm, Tues, Wed, Fri, Sat
10 am-6 pm, Sun 12 pm-5 pm
CC: A, M, V

If you like stuffed animals, or want a unique gift for someone who does, this is the place to find teddy bears, rhinos, monkeys, fawns, seals, bunnies, pigs, lambs, ducks, zebras, panthers and 3-humped camels. You may walk in a hardened sophisticate, but you could just as easily walk out with a new pet under your arm, chosen from this great collection of quality stuffed animals from companies all over the world: American Gund, German Steiff, which produced the original teddy bear and Italian Avanti, which makes perfect replicas including details from eyelashes to cloven hooves. Prices start at $4 and go to $3000 for a giant polar bear. The widest selection is in the $30 to $50 range.

Toward the back of the shop you will find a number of Madame Alexander dolls, collector's items, with china faces and moveable eyes, which cost around $400. Other magnificent dolls and puppets dressed in creamy antique lace and ribbons are made by Louis Nichole, the interior decorator. The Camille ballerina marionette is breathtakingly realistic and the Merlin doll, with its billowy beard and shiny blue robes, is charming. -JJ

BEGGAR'S MARKET LTD.

15 E Chestnut / 60611   944-1835
Hours: Mon, Tues, Wed, Fri 11 am–7 pm, Sat 12 pm–
5:30 pm, Sun 12 pm–4 pm
CC: A, M, V

Everything in this little shop in the Chestnut Street Galleria is beautifully crafted from the best natural materials, whether it's jewelry, clothes or ceramics, and the selection can suit tastes running from rustic to sophisticated. In the front of the shop are display cases filled with dolls with life-like porcelain faces and dresses of gauze, lamé or wool, and with glasses and paperweights of murrini glass made by an ancient technique which creates lovely and unique effects. Farther back in the store is a display of Japanese tableware: delicate dishes in dark colors are beautiful as well as practical.

Jewelry ranges from trendy to nostalgic, at prices from moderate to expensive. Earrings, of which there is a large selection, range from $20 to $50, in bright enamels, glass geometrics, porcelain, gold abstracts and a popular series made of blown glass and silver filigree. There are also vintage pieces, including carnelian and rose quartz necklaces. Then there are some distinctive small finger rings with opals, lapis and diamonds, priced from $65 to $300.

Angora and silk shawls abound here, in pastels and earth tones ($50), and so do sweaters, hats and scarves, all handmade. There are conversation piece T-shirts and sweatshirts, both domestic and Italian ($13 to $26), and hand-made children's clothes, including a tiny lace-covered christening gown. Some of the most charming items in the store, and certainly some of the best buys, is a line of leather infant's and toddler's shoes called Storkenworks, made by a husband and wife, in red, white and mauve, at $15 a pair. Jeanine told me that one customer bought enough pairs to keep her friend's newborn in Storkenworks until she was two. What a lucky kid!

Finally, there is a large selection of cards, stationery, mailable children's books and other small gifts that can brighten someone's day without emptying anyone's pockets. –JJ

BENETTON'S

608 N Michigan / 60611   944-2904
2828 N Clark (Century Mall) / 60657   972-7111
121 E Oak / 60611   944-0434
25 E Washington / 60602   855-0775
Water Tower Place: 835 N Michigan / 60611
337-3901
Hours: (Michigan Ave store only. Call for other stores.):
Mon–Fri 10 am–8 pm, Sat 10 am–6 pm, Sun 11 am–
5 pm
CC: A, M, V

This chain features soft, oversized sweater clothes in bright colors. Franchise stores are popping up like mushrooms all over the city: everything in all of them carries the Italian Benetton label but stock varies with the individual taste of each store's buyer. When I visited the one on Michigan Ave., it was filled with an after-work crowd of shoppers, including young and young-at-heart women, all being helped by enthusiastic salespeople. One 40-ish customer said happily, "I've never worn red before!"

All clothes have Italian sizes, but the staff are happy to help you find what fits. In any case, many clothes come in small, medium and large sizes only. A typical wool pullover in a rainbow choice of colors runs about $50, and a matching skirt with an elastic waist and polyester lining is $60. A crisp cotton blouse with a Peter Pan collar, designed to be layered by vests, cardigans and/or pullovers, runs $30. For $55 you can buy a terrific heavy-duty blue denim jacket and there are short jackets and calf-length coats in royal blue and white. Look too for rugby shirts, oversized cotton flannel patterned shirts, Benetton sweatsuits and stirrups, in wool and cotton and many colors. These sweater clothes are carried year 'round. It will be hard to put them aside when the weather heats up. –JJ

BOUTIQUE CAPRICE

47 W Division / 60610   943-6993
Hours: Mon–Fri. 10 am–7 pm, Sat 10 am–6 pm, Sun 11 am–5 pm
CC: A, D, M, V

Most of the clothes here are designed to take you through a business day and straight out to dinner at any elegant restaurant. You can find lots of dresses, both for day and evening. There is a nice selection of bright and colorful silks and hand-beaded and sequined evening dresses. Bright colors are one of the things this shop stands for: fuschias, greens and teal blues—along with more sedate taupes and browns, of course. Jhane Barnes suits are here in rainbow-colored tweeds ($200 to $400). Also Vakko colorful, well-made leather jackets, pants and mix and match separates. Sizes in the shops are 7 to 14. Boutique Caprice prides itself not only on its colorful merchandise, but on supplying business suits and wool dresses that can go to the office, as well as its appealing evening wear. There are clutches and handbags here, too, some imported from Italy, that run from about $50 to $120, and you can buy a silk hand-beaded evening bag ($60 to $100) to go out to dinner with you. You can find winter and summer coats here, something that every boutique does not carry. And there are shoes: two-toned trendy pumps with removable metallic decoration ($110), both reptile and plain leather shoes in 15 fashion colors ($80 to $150). And socks and pantyhose—lacy and textured. And stockings, some of which are very fancy, and which too are often hard to find. Barbara, the manager, says that all the sales assistants have professional fashion training and will spend whatever time with you that you need to help you with your purchasing decisions. –MC

BURDI

68 E Walton / 60611   642-9166/9167
Hours: Mon–Sat 10 am–6 pm, Closed Sun
CC: A, M, V

The *Dynasty* look is hot at this designer shop. For Joan Collins and all other size sevens there is a black velvet lamé suit with a fitted skirt ($1,225), a pillbox hat with a veil ($100), and beautiful crepe, lamé, georgette and silk dresses ($350 to $1000). For spring, Burdi has lovely linen blouses ($200) and sophisticated town suits in silk and linen blends ($500).

In the men's department you can find Zegna lightweight wool and silk-blend suits from Italy ($625), soft Swiss cotton day and formal shirts ($80 to $135) and elegant custom-made sports jackets which begin at $750. A cloth or leather jacket by Mario Valentine

put together with Burdi's European style wool blend slacks will run you about $1000. And there are Italian and French silk ties at $45. This shop is obviously expensive, but the clothing is unusually stylish and good quality. Celebrities shop here—Brooke Shields for one, and Cubs outfielder Davey Lopes for another.
-MC

CHIÁSSO

13 E Chestnut / 60611   642-2808
Hours: Mon, Tues, Wed, Fri 11 am–7 pm, Thurs 11 am–8 pm, Sat 10 am–6 pm, Sun 12 pm–5 pm
CC: A, M, V

Here is where you can get "functional art"—office accessories, toys, games, gadgets, utensils and some furniture—by American and European designers. Everything is high tech in black, white, red and grey, with sleek geometric lines. There is a wide price range, and this is a great place to find gifts. Try buying someone the "Penultimate": a clear plastic pen with a zigzag yellow clip and green and pink pyramids and other doodads on top, which goes for $3. At the other end of the price scale, $800 will buy you a white enamel clock from Japan, with little antennae positioned around its face, in lieu of a second hand, which vibrate one after another to mark the seconds. In between you can spend $60 for a watch by Ixis with a plastic band—$220 will get you one with a pigskin band. Or look for the wooden Italian Hat Trees with colored wooden screw-on hats that you can change with the seasons—grays for winter, pastels for spring. And bright plastic shaving brushes and razors to wake you up on dreary mornings. Then there are dominoes, chess sets, drinking glasses, corkscrews, swizzle sticks, lamps, scissors, paperclip holders, bar stools, cards and stationery—all interesting designs.

Chiásso also carries jewelry handmade by several artists. Most of it is rather expensive. Pieces by Dutch artist Hans Appenzeller include his silver-folded moon earrings ($140) and metal grid earrings which look like loosely woven cloth ($170). Ulrike Knab, a German artist, is represented by single earrings: one is called "Explosion". Unlike a conventional earring, it juts forward from the ear and the effect is startling. Knab also does interesting pieces in slate, and iron embedded in steel. Her work runs around $150.

Anyone with a taste for quality, trendiness and plain fun will love Chiásso. -JJ

CITY

213 W Institute Place / 60610   664-9581
Hours: Mon–Sat: 10 am–6 pm, Sun 12 pm–5 pm
CC: A, M, V

This is a selective high-tech specialty shop selling unusual clothing and jewelry, linens and soaps, Italian furniture and elegant office supplies, including pens. It's fun to browse at City after a delicious lunch at Monique's Cafe next door in the same building which is a beautifully rehabbed old factory. The clothing section offers superb loose-fitting cotton shirts, pants and skirts, which show the strong influence of Japanese style trends. There are extra short and extra long skirts and trendy jewelry, scarves and some handbags to go with them. Prices are high, but they compare favorably with prices in New York, San

Francisco and Los Angeles. In the furniture section you will see unique sofas, chairs, lamps and clocks. Everything is sleek and expensive. The linens and shower curtains come in fashionable grey, white, black and red. I really love the desk accessories: colorful plastic paper-clips, shelves, paper trays, notebooks, portfolios and imported pens. City has a loft look and whether you live in one or not, this is a perfect place to shop. –MC

CRATE & BARREL

850 N Michigan / 60611   787-5900
Hours: Mon & Thurs 10 am–7 pm, T, W, F & Sat 10 am–6 pm, Sunday 12 pm–5 pm
101 N Wabash / 60602   372-0100
Hours: Mon–Sat 10 am–6 pm, Closed Sun
1510 N Wells St / 60610 ("Outlet" Store)   787-4775
Hours: Mon 10 am–7 pm, Tues–Sa. 10 am–6 pm, Sunday 12 pm–5 pm
(All stores) CC: A, M, V

Since Gordon and Carole Segal founded C&B in 1962, it has become a kind of retailing institution which specializes in kitchen, cooking and entertainment ware.

You'll find a wide variety of glass and stemware, ceramics, silverware and kitchen aids to satisfy the most fastidious gourmet. In fact, this is a gadgeteer's paradise: bottles and jars for many purposes, knives galore, corkscrews, decanters and stacking baskets which can be used in the kitchen, the den, the bedroom. What's nice about shopping here, in fact, is that many of the items have dual or triple purposes and can be adapted to virtually any decor, although basically the look is clean, uncluttered and elegant modern.

While all three stores tend to stock more or less the same merchandise, Wells Street doubles as a sort of clearance center, not only for closeouts from their other shops, but also for manufacturers' end-of-line and discontinued merchandise. So you'll find many bargains at Wells Street in slightly damaged glassware (sometimes so slight as to be undetectable), dishes and other ceramic pieces. And there are often specials on rugs.

In addition, there are selections of Marimekko bedding, pillows, carry bags and purses. The stores almost always feature sturdy, simple leather bags and brief cases which are very smart and usually come in a blond finish; there are also canvas bags and cases, many by Marimekko. Crate & Barrel also carries furniture (outdoor, children's, office) and sleek desk accessories, including notebooks and ball point pens.

All of the stores have the same high tech, yet warm and woody look: plain, polished wood floors and brick walls give the atmosphere a feeling of spaciousness. And you can find goods from $1-$100 after you've finished browsing. –EM

DEI GIOVANI

1205 N State Pkway / 60610   787-5239
Hours: Mon–Sat 11 am–7 pm, Sun 12 am–5 pm
2421 N Clark / 60614   549-4116
Hours: Mon–Fri 12 pm–8 pm, Sat 11 am–7 pm, Sun 12 pm–5 pm
CC: A, C, D, M, V

Dei Giovani's forte is the elegant look for men. Here you can buy exclusive Italian clothing designed by Lorenz Nicola, and the price range is broad. There are linen and cotton dress and everyday shirts ($30 to $165), hand-made wool, alpaca and mohair-and-silk blend sweaters ($150 to $400) and jerseys and flat knits ($30 to $250). There is a large stock of elegant suits made of wool-silk-cotton-linen blends; the prices range between $275 and $800. Silk ties run $15 to $50. Manager Nick Furio says that the look for '86 will be oversized, and consequently Dei Giovani has lots of wool-linen-cotton blend loose-fitting sports coats and somewhat baggy slacks, and full raincoats in natural colors from Germany and Italy ($300-$400). If you buy a sport coat, slacks, matching shirt and tie here you will spend between $400 and $1000 for your ensemble. But Nick and his staff have a terrific color sense so you can trust them to mix and match your day and evening looks with the greatest of care. –MC

ENCHANTÉ

Water Tower Place: 835 N Michigan / 60611
951-7290
Hours: Mon & Thurs 10 am–7 pm, Tues, Wed, Fri,
Sat 10 am–6 pm, Sun 12 pm–5 pm
CC: A, C, D, M, V

The specialty here is designer lingerie, some of which is imported especially for this shop from France and Italy. Enchanté has the largest silk lingerie collection in Chicago, the owner says. There are matching silk camisoles and tap pants, pretty extra-long and short mini slips in pastel colors and beautifully-made silk underwire bras from France. You can buy bras, panties, teddies, robes, pajamas and gowns in satin as well as silk. There are blends of cotton and silk which are somewhat less expensive than the silk varieties: cotton and silk knit Hanro and Ripcosa camisoles are attractive. The owner of this shop does not wish prices to be printed, but I can tell you that these blended camisoles sell for under $100. Other accessories include silk stockings, self-conscious fluffy high-heeled mules and ballet shoes in paisley prints and subtle floral patterns. –MC

END OF THE LINE

8 E Chestnut / 60611   951-0136
Hours: Mon–Fri 11 am–7 pm, Sat 10 am–6 pm, Closed Sun
CC: A, M, V

This fairly new shop, tucked into a little stone row house across the street from the Chestnut Street Galleria, offers a nice selection of brilliant casual clothes. Anne Pinkerton is well represented, with mammoth rayon blouses in white and shimmery gold ($80) and coordinating black pants and vests. There are stirrup pants and oversized patterned blouses For layering over everything you can find Anne Pinkerton's oversized sweaters in tweeds with flecks of pink, red and turquoise for $138. A wild new line by Camps features black and turquoise warm-up pants and padded jackets printed to look something like rock. Store manager Wendy Potter calls it "the Rambo Look". These clothes run big in all sizes and most are designed to fit loosely. There is a small selection of costume jewelry.

In warmer weather expect the same, lightened up to beat the heat. –JJ

ETCETERA

Water Tower Place: 835 N Michigan / 60611
944-0405
Hours: Mon, Thurs 10 am–7 pm, Tues, Wed, Fri, Sat
10 am–6 pm, Sun 12 am–5 pm
CC: A, M, V

You want a pink flamingo bedside lamp? A Betty Boop plate? How about a life-sized Gumby, a Groucho Marx puppet or a watch that looks like a car with a hood that opens to display the date? All this—and more—is at Joann Rockman's toy store for adults. After 10 years in the business—8 of them at this location—Joann still enjoys talking about the man who bought himself a teddy bear and the woman who bought two "rock" purses—they look like rocks with shoulder straps—and planned to hang one on the wall. Then there are her friends who supply her with stock: the man who has been traveling to Indonesia since his hippie days to bring her fantastic Balinese ceremonial masks, and the other friend who provides reproductions of Art Deco lamps, tables and ornaments and who has built himself a guitar-shaped swimming pool with the proceeds. She can tell you also about the locally-made Silvestri reproductions of Egyptian glass she sells. They are rough-finished, graceful and iridescent, and much cheaper than the real thing. Prices throughout the store are moderate.

Take a look at the jewelry cases. There are earrings and necklaces made of chunky, faceted false gemstones, as well as plastic cars and trucks on little black plastic chains. More elegant are a wonderful collection of enamel earrings by a company called A Thousand Flowers ($15 to $20). And there are brass, gold, silver and iridescent metallic earrings, at moderate prices, some made by local artists.

This delightful miscellany will provide something to please any grown-up kid. –JJ

FLY-BY-NITE GALLERY

714 N Wells / 60614   664-8136
Hours: Mon–Sat 10 am–5 pm or by app't.
CC: Cash Or Check Only

Thomas Tomc thinks of himself as the proprietor of a kind of gallery, rather than a shop; his stock is a collection rather than an inventory. He has been in business in the same location for 23 years. His specialty is Art Nouveau—Jungendstil and European arts and crafts—and Art Deco. He sells mirrors, pottery, vases, paintings, posters, etchings, candelabras, furniture, wood carvings and jewelry. Most of this is imported from Europe and the majority of the imports are from France. His Art Nouveau vases run $200 to $3000. He has 1000 pieces of European ceramics dating from 1900 to 1930, and he has graphics and lithographs from that period as well. In the jewelry case are necklaces, pins, rings, pendants, earrings, bracelets, mostly of silver in a price range from $75 to $750. I saw exquisite Finnish silver bracelets with gemstones from the '50s ($125-$500). Fly-By-Nite has the largest collection of its type in the United States. Ninety-five percent of the items in this gallery are catalogued and a card attached to each piece gives its origin as well as its price. Often Tom can give you a complete history of the object, but he is straightforward about it if he has no information. He makes frequent trips to Europe and also receives constant additions to his stock from European sources. –MC

HANDLE WITH CARE

1706 N Wells / 60614   751-2929
Hours: Mon–Fri 10 am–6:30 pm, Sat 10 am–6 pm, Sun 12 pm–5 pm
CC: A, M, V

Jan Pomerantz, the owner of this boutique, with its subdued lighting and khaki color scheme, sells charming clothes with careful detailing that are never boring. The look here is one of easy chic. A good example is the Dorothee Bis line which Jan discovered on one of her trips to Paris. There are brightly colored linen separates which sell for about $200 an outfit: the long, narrow skirts look great with matching midriff sweaters and oversized blazers. If you don't like body-hugging clothes, Dorothee Bis has "big" dresses that look attractive either belted or worn loose with pumps.

There are other loose dresses made by Tod Oldham; these seem deceptively demure but have surprising details: a low-cut back, for instance ($100 to $200). Original, creative clothes by Chicago designers are not cheap ($200 to $300), but are classic designs that are really well-made and will look good for many seasons, so they are worth the price. This shop is known for its sweaters, most of which are handmade. We saw one by Dorothee Bis in soft cotton: it was beige with a black knitted face on the front and small black number on the back ($300). The average price for Jan's sweaters is $150, with a good selection available in all seasons.

Unusual lingerie and nightwear can also be found here. And it would be easy to become addicted to a line of underwear by Hanro, a Swiss company. For mother and baby there are lovely hand-beaded and hand-embroidered undershirts and panties by Marybeth (mom's set: $68; baby's: $30). One undershirt had shoulderpads sewn in, a clever way to update a dress or suit ($36). And Handle With Care has accessories. Scarves, belts, Hue socks and tights and sharp hats by David and Hat Attack. And a sensational jewelry section. Jan goes as far afield as Paris (and as near as Chicago) to acquire stunning earrings, bracelets and necklaces. A pair of earrings could run as high as $100, but each design is unique.

If you are looking for soaps, lotions, shampoos or potpourri, you can find lines here like Caswell-Massey, Roget and Rigaud. And as if this weren't enough, they also sell leather wallets and address books and little novelties like a suede hippo which we admired; it was $22. These nice touches make the boutique all the more inviting. Jan does a terrific job of providing clothes and accessories that will never bore you. –AT

IN RARE FORM
814 N Franklin / 60610   944-0069
Hours: Mon–Sat, 10 am–6 pm, Sun, 12 pm–5 pm
Closed Mon
CC: A, M, V

This fashion-forward men's shop in the same building as the Raccoon Club, is one of the new retail establishments which are springing up in the burgeoning rehabbed Near North area along the El tracks. Women too can wear most of these clothes, so in a sense the shop is unisex.

Owners Jim Green and Jeff Mayer feature Perry Ellis and Jhane Barnes designs as well as work by European couturiers: sweaters, shirts, pants, sweatshirts, and unstructured sportcoats in small, medium and large sizes. You can buy an elegant sweater for as little as $65; the handmade ones, which are even more elegant, go for $135-$300. The designs are striking and the materials include cotton, wool and silk, some blends, some pure and simple.

The shop itself is pleasantly spacious (some 3000 sq. ft.), and its minimalist appointments and natural materials contribute an air of opulence and modernity. –EM

INTRINSIC

440 N Wells / 60610   644-6212
Hours: Mon–Fri 11 am–7 pm, Sat 10 am–6 pm, Sun 12 pm–5 pm
CC: A, M, V

Cary Fetman believed that Chicago had a crying need for a with-it store where men could find the kind of personal service that women have always enjoyed. So he opened the very "in" Intrinsic in 1983. This is the place to go for the distinctive and the outrageous in men's fine fashions. Merchandise begins with the basics, and grows more intriguing with one-of-a-kind shirts and sweaters, culminating in accessories like scarves and pins. Prices are in the upper range, since Intrinsic offers the work of top designers who tend to use leather, silk and other expensive materials.

Cary and his creative staff cater to each customer's needs and tastes, and they always bear in mind that most men are not familiar with forward fashions. When you enter the shop, you receive a friendly greeting and you can have plenty of explanations of how to coordinate your clothes and your accessories. If that word "accessories" frightens you fellows, you can calm down because everything at Intrinsic is designed for men. Of course Cary is the first to acknowledge that 60% of the sales are to women who are buying for their men or for themselves.

People-watching is fun at Intrinsic. You might run into your doctor, looking at a Philippe Monet jacket that you're considering for yourself. A commodities broker can be seen carrying a Cynthia Szato appliqued jacket into a dressing room, where the booth next door is occupied by a chic woman slipping into a La Matta shirt in a small size. Of course gay men find a congenial home here, as do celebrities from all over the country. Bulls star Reggie Theus shops here, and so does all-star wrestler Spike Huber, as well as Chili Pepper, the female impersonator. When Prince was in town he came here, and Alice Cooper and Tony Geary are among Cary's customers. Oprah Winfrey often wears Cary's fashions on her show.

You'll also find accessories for women as well as unisex accessories, and jewelry by Wendy Gail which runs from $20 to $1500.

Anything that appeals to Cary can end up as stock such as leather teddy bears and Mandarin Duck luggage. Designers are Mario Valentino, Gianni Versace, Claude Montana, Umberto Ginocchitti and the more subdued Zanella. But don't let these names intimidate you: Cary and his staff will let you choose those items which will help awaken the desire for adventure that slumbers in all of us. –AT

JEAN CHARLES LA MODE A DEUX

30 E Oak / 60611 (Shoes)   787-3535
1003 N Rush / 60611 (Clothing)   787-3535
Hours: Mon–Sat 10 am–6:30 pm, Sun 12 pm–5 pm
CC: A, D, M, V

In this shop you will find imported clothing and shoes for men and women. The shoes and clothing shops have different addresses, but are actually physically connected. In the shoe store you will find items like brightly colored handmade shoes from René Caty in France at a price between $160 and $190, reptile pumps and calfskin high-heeled pumps by Gino Aldrovandi starting at $165, and—most unusual—flats by the Japanese designer Tokyo Kumagai decorated with animal motifs. My favorite is decorated with mice and comes in black and grey leather at $125. You can also find "mood shoes" here: these high-throated pumps change color, going from black to navy to bright blue as your feet warm up during the course of the day. They start at $110—pricey for a conversation piece, but they are attractive. More conservative hand-woven unisex leather loafers in natural colors are yours for $200. For men only there are heavy-soled Japanese walking shoes for $195. Most of these designs are exclusives here. There are woven leather Stephane Kehan shoes for men.

In the clothing store are unisex leather jackets printed with flowers in pastels and natural colors, and bright (even orange) raincoats with huge lapels for about $400. For the Miami Vice Look, try a unisex Adolfo Dominguez suit with an over-sized jacket for $800. Navy blue coats and jackets in a gabardine-and-wool blend by the French designer Marthe Françoise Girbaud, also unisex, sell for $600 to $1000.

Flatware, china and crystal by Jean Charles de Castlebajac are also for sale here: the delicate place settings are displayed in a glass case exactly as they were shown at the Museum of Modern Art in Paris in 1984. They are beautiful but extremely expensive and must be special ordered. So plan several weeks ahead for the next royal wedding. –MC

A JOINT VENTURE

1704 N Wells / 60614   440-0505
Hours: Mon–Fri 11 am–6:30 pm, Sat 10 am–5 pm, Sun 12 pm–4 pm
CC: A

The owners of this beautiful gift shop, Fred Gardner and Joseph Lopresti, travel far and wide to find unusual paintings, jewelry, toys and greeting cards. In the gallery section are art objects from Europe and the Orient. Many of these are one-of-a kind and they are not cheap. Occasionally A Joint Venture gets a limited shipment of European Deco and printing art. You might want to put yourself on their mailing list. –MC

LATHAM LIMITED

509 W Diversey / 60614   248-3464
1133 N State / 60610   787-9349
(See listing under Mid North)

LORI'S DESIGNER SHOES

808 W Armitage / 60614   281-5655

*Hours: Mon–Thurs 11 am–7 pm, Fri & Sat 11 am–6 pm,
Sun 12 pm–5 pm*
CC: A, M, V

Here is where you can buy designer shoes, boots and handbags at genuine discount prices. Lori Neu buys up merchandise being sold off, for whatever reason, by factories and sells it at a 20% to 60% discount. The setting is no frills, but there is personalized service. Customers get the attention they need. Lori likes to say that people come in as customers and walk out as friends. Shoe sizes run from 5½ to 10, and widths as narrow as double A are offered. You can buy pantyhose here too, and knee highs. There is a unique selection of tights in unusual patterns from various manufacturers. Some have been discontinued. I bought two pairs of designer casual shoes here for $100 and checked them out elsewhere, to find that they were retailing at more than $160 each. The selection of handbags is small, but the leather is very high quality and most are Italian imports. You can get good style and quality at Lori's for a good price. –MC

MARY WALTER

300 W Grand / 60611   661-1094
*Hours: Mon–Fri 10 am–6 pm, Sat 10 am–5 pm, Closed
Sun*
CC: A, M, V

The salespeople here are wardrobe specialists who enjoy helping customers select the right clothes for their business and personal lives. They encourage you to bring in some of your own clothes to make sure that your new purchases will blend in with your wardrobe, since the emphasis here is on quality (expensive) garments that are neither trendy nor ultra-conservative, that will mix and match with separates already in your closet and fit in with your life style. A card is made listing your tastes in style and color and kept to provide information for anyone who wants to buy you a gift.

This formula has worked so well in Mary Walter's two Evanston stores that she has transformed this shop in the Off Center Mall from an outlet into a full-fledged store. The clientele are upwardly mobile career women of all ages. Sizes range from 4 to 14, with a few things coming in larger and smaller sizes. The clothes generally tend to run full. Small women will find petite sizes scattered throughout the shop.

Clothes are displayed in groupings to help you see how colors and separates can be used together. I saw one corner holding groupings of separates in burgundy, gray and cream, another in red, black, yellow and dark green, and still another in bright green, yellow, pink and purple.

There are tailored two-piece suits by Cricketeer and Harry Bricker in navy and heather blue, grey, black and muted plaids; they are impeccably made and run around $450. Jeremiah, another major line, is more casual with bolder colors and weaves; Mary Walter recommends it for leisure wear or for women in advertising or creative careers. I saw a wonderful wool and cashmere camel sports jacket for $240. To complement these clothes there is a large selection of blouses both in cotton, polyester and silk for day, and rich embossed silk for evening ($40 to $100).

I visited in Fall when there was a nice selection of resort and holiday wear: Merona cotton sweaters, culottes and polo shirts in jewel colors, flowered cotton shirtwaist dresses, pink, green and turquoise velvet and black reversible jackets and black velvet pants. In warmer months these things come in silk, linen and cotton. You can also find accessories—shoes, belts and scarves—and a small selection of jewelry, some handmade by local artists. –JJ

MY SISTER'S CIRCUS / ISIS

38 E Oak / 60611   664-7076/7074
Hours: Mon–Fri 10:30 am–7 pm, Sat 10 am–6 pm, Sun 12 pm–5 pm
CC: Cash Or Check Only

This shop is practically a Chicago landmark, having been owned by Suzanne Gantz for nearly 20 years. Gwen, the manager, has been here for 13 of those years. The specialty is one-size-fits-almost-all casual clothing with a distinctive look. There are only three lines of clothing sold here: Michelle Lamay and Tornado from California, and Liase Adzer from Morocco. The Lamay and Adzer clothes are exclusive here; they cannot be bought anywhere else in town. Pants, skirts, tops, jackets and dresses come in more than a dozen colors and are made of easy-care cotton and rayon in knits, and smooth and tweedy fabrics. Prices are moderate, ranging from $40 to $300. I really like the oversized jackets and cotton and wool handwoven overpieces. You can buy fringed scarves to match your outfit for about $15. Year 'round this store stocks cruisewear so that lightweight clothing is always available for your vacation. The jewelry department is called Isis: here you will find the exclusive work of several talented Chicago designers. Handcrafted belts and earrings are priced between $40 and $200. Beverly Crown and Oprah Winfrey shop here; they like the look and the comfort of the clothes. Several times Suzanne has tried to shut the shop and retire but her customers have forced her to relent and keep on going. Drop in here to find out why. –MC

ONE PLUS ONE

Wearable Addition
815 W Armitage / 60614   975-8559
Hours: Tues–Sat 11 am–6 pm, Sun 10 am–5 pm
Closed Mon
CC: M, V

This unique little shop, situated on the ground floor of an old two-story apartment building, features "modular clothing": tops, skirts and pants in vibrant gem colors to be mixed and matched. And whether you're a petite size 2 or a sumptuous 20, one size fits all. How is this possible? By using matching bandeaux ($5) you can belt these contemporary garments to fit your own shape. Even pregnant women find these clothes especially appealing. Proprietor-Designer Stefani Bay opened her store about a year ago to sell the kinds of clothing and accessories she herself likes, and at prices virtually anyone can handle: nothing in the store sells for more than $50.

All garments are made in Chicago of cotton and polyester and are washable. Skirts and tops range from $25-$48 and the thermal quality of the knitwear makes it comfortable for all seasons. There is a neat collection of suede handmade neckpieces—a sort of combination ascot and bandana in an assortment of colors—for $24. At the same price there are hand-

43

painted scarves. For only $5 you can get a cleverly expandable piece which can be a dickie or can stretch easily into a headband or hood for outdoor wear: slip it back around your neck and it's a turtle neck again. It comes in a variety of colors.

There is a fairly good selection of jewelry ($5.50-$50): earrings and large necklaces and a range of bracelets. The accessories are also designer pieces, but, unlike the clothes, these are supplied by artisans from all over the US.

One Plus One, with its bare wooden floors, white walls and white wire baskets filled with one-size-fits-all goodies, is a charming and satisfying place to get fit without exerting yourself. –EM

OVER THE RAINBOW

Water Tower Place: 835 N Michigan / 60611
943-2050
Hours: Mon & Thurs 10 am–7 pm, Tues, Wed, Fri,
Sat 10 am–6 pm, Sun 12 pm–5 pm
CC: A, D, M, V

In this cute little shop for tots, Karen DeFelippi sells very expensive but delightful clothes, shoes and accessories for newborns to five-year-olds—infant to size 6. There are pink satin jumpsuits ($54), little sneakers by Coveri in bright solids and prints ($35), patent leather dress slippers with rhinestones by Little Flirts ($40) and the ultimate grandmother gift: Italian velvet or silk floral dresses with lace collars ($200-$250). There is also a line of Japanese sportswear for children by Kido: baggy pants, oversized jackets, shirts, accessories, socks, belts—all of which can be coordinated to give your toddler that total look for nursery school. Right now pastel colors are hot for little girls. -MC

PAPER & COMPANY

100 E Walton / 60611   440-0696
Hours: Mon–Fri 10 am–6 pm, Sat 9:30 am–5:30 pm,
Closed Sun
CC: M, V

Greeting cards, invitations, gift wrapping, party plates and napkins, decorations, personalized note pads...You name it. They have it. This new stationery and paper goods store even has bulk supplies for corporate parties with 16 solid colors and 40 prints to choose from. There is personalized stationary ($25 for 50 sheets with envelopes); shopping bags in dozens of colors and sizes (.75¢ to $3); paper guest towels ($1.75 to $3 a package) and place cards and mats, doilies, invitations and decorations at varying prices. If you want special party goods for any special occasion or holiday Paper & Co. will accept special orders; and owners Donna Sloan and Robert Stitzberg will work with you. You can find a lot of attractive bread-and-butter gifts here at between $5 and $10—not unreasonable for this pricey part of town. -MC

PAVO REAL

Water Tower Place: 835 N Michigan / 60611
944-1390
Hours: Mon & Thurs 10 am–7 pm, Tues, Wed, Fri, Sat
10 am–6 pm, Sun 12 pm –5 pm
CC: A, M, V

This shop sells, among other things, work by Sergio

Bustamente, the Mexican artist. There are lovely, brilliantly colored papier maché animals in many sizes, some made to hang from the ceiling—zebras, armadillos, parrots and tigers, all originals and all very expensive. There is a thriving business in Mexico in copies of Bustamente's work, as anyone knows who has been there. Pavo Real is divided into a gallery and a boutique: two different stores, the manager says, in one store. The boutique sells Latin American woven sashes, shawls, tapestry bags, rugs, blankets, wall hangings and handwoven garments for men and women at prices from $70 to $150. Cotton and alpaca sweaters from Mexico and Peru (starting around $30) are attractively displayed next to Bustamente's works and the effect is striking and original. Some of Bustamente's new work is brass and copper. Pavo Real is a small chain, with stores in New York, Boston and Washington, D.C. as well as Chicago. –MC

PRIMITIVE ARTS LTD

Water Tower Place: 835 N Michigan / 60611
337-2011
Hours: Mon & Thurs 10 am–7 pm, Tues, Wed, Fri, Sat
10 am–6 pm, Sun 12 pm–5 pm
CC: M, V

This shop is located near the movie theatres on the second level of Water Tower Place. The emphasis is on imports but recently trendy gifts have been added to the stock—baskets, pottery, and all sorts of charming little things, like Chinese pin cushions which come in all sizes, prices starting at $1.50. Lacquer boxes from India cost $5 to $10. There are a few art objects from Africa and lots of Mexican rugs and Peruvian wall hangings in various sizes—one beautiful large wall hanging goes for $650. The jewelry section is eclectic. Silver hoops and post earrings from Mexico are reasonably priced and there are reproductions of Art Deco: pins, earrings, necklaces ($8 to $40). -MC

RECREATIONS MATERNITY SHOP

Chestnut Street Galleria: 17 E Chestnut (2nd floor) /
60611   664-1840
Hours: Mon–Fri 10 am–7 pm, Thurs 10 am–8 pm, Sat
10 am–6 pm, Sun 12 pm–5 pm
CC: A, M, V

This is a branch of a national chain which specializes in practical but pretty and moderately-priced maternity wear. There is a career section with suits which start at $100 and smart daytime dresses at $80 and up. Also at $80 are pretty paisley cotton dresses which can go through any season and are appropriate for almost any occasion. There are colorful patterned wool and acrylic sweaters ($30 to $60), and comfortable cotton turtlenecks ($33) and blouses in prints and solid ($40), both of which can be worn with jumpsuits and overalls, or with elastic-waisted pants ($30). For special occasions you can get a velvet evening dress for $165. A real blessing are maternity pantyhose ($4.50 to $7.50) and hard-to-find leotards ($38). Pick up a mail order catalogue while you're here, and you might want to stop in for a tasty snack at the Convito Italiano restaurant next door. -MC

ROWBOTTOMS AND WILLOUGHBY'S OUTFITTERS

72 W Hubbard / 60610   329-0999

Hours: Mon, Tues, Wed, Fri 10 am–6 pm, Thurs 10 am–7:30 pm, Sat 10 am–5 pm
CC: A, M, V

You can find the original Hemingway jacket and Lindberg coat, and leather A-Z and G-1 flight jackets here, a stone's throw from the Merchandise Mart, along with all kinds of English, Australian, New Zealand and American field wear. This two-year-old store, owned by Jerry and Debby Brody, features the top-of-the-line in traditional outerwear, not only for real-life hunters, fishermen and trappers, but for armchair and urban sportspeople as well. Outside the store you will be greeted by a full-sized plastic horse covered by a wool blanket. Inside, there is rustic comfort: the clothes lie on tables or are tucked into antique English pine cupboards (for sale on consignment), and hang on some racks. Debbie and Jerry are on hand to advise, and there is Irish music by the Chieftains.

In the men's section is almost a complete line of Barbour, a hundred-year-old company offering oil-cloth field coats which really smell oily ($225) and other "Best British Clothes for the Worst English Weather". There are honest-to-goodness mackintoshes here from John Calder, another British company ($155) and you can also find a complete line of Willis and Jackson who turn out, in addition to flight jackets, whipcord trousers and jackets and quail coats, with lots of interesting pockets and zippers. Sweaters in all sizes and shapes start around $65; many are extra-heavy, and oiled to keep out the elements. Wool and moleskin shirts start at about $50. And these things are in stock year 'round, along with rugby shirts and shorts, running pants and polo shirts.

All this clothing may be worn by women, too, but Rowbottoms' women's department has been expanded to fill about 40% of the space, and offers a large line of clothes by Ruff Hewn and British Khaki, which has boot-length wool and corduroy skirts in muted tweeds, plaids and earth tones, and blue denim gaucho skirts. There are blouses with unusual detailing in bold plaids and pastels by Eileen West and Norman ($50) and bulky, luscious sweaters ($80 up) and vests ($60) from Peru. From Chile come handspun knit sweaters in vibrant shades of pink, green and turqoise: vests are $60, cardigans are $110. These woolens are carried the year 'round, with some seasonal fluctuation, and, in general, women's clothes are sized to fit more trimly than men's, and the women's department puts more emphasis on fashion than on comfort in the wild.

This shop also stocks a complete line of riding wear for both men and women, and small accessories like jewelry, scarves, perfume, socks, gloves, umbrellas, canvas totes, corkscrews, and even the ubiquitous Swiss Army knife. –JJ

S'AGARO

1712 N Wells / 60614   944-6732
Hours: Mon–Fri 10 am–6:30 pm, Sat 10 am–6 pm, Sun 12 pm–5 pm
CC: A, M, V

This new women's shoe boutique, named after a resort in southern Spain, is owned by mother and daughter Gloria and Martha Turner. Gloria minds the store while Martha attends Barnard College and takes buying trips to Spain and Italy. The shop has imported boots, flats and low-to-mid heels in several colors and textures at moderate prices: $65 to $100. The emphasis here is on comfort: the Turners believe that high heels are bad for you, and they have set out to prove that you can look stylish and attractive in low or mid (2 inch) heels. They have trendy metallics and suedes and platform shoes with thick soles. Flats designed by Chicagoan Von Mon are very comfortable, come in natural colors and cost about $65. Perfect for these shoes are colorful textured tights, knee highs and anklets from the Sox Trot Company, priced between $3.50 and $15. There is a small but unusual selection of handbags, most of which are very large and made of soft leather and fabrics. Prices for them start at $80. The decor here is uncluttered and attractive, and the service is excellent. -MC

STAARA

1711 N Halsted / 60614   280-1832
Hours: Mon–Fri 12 pm–8 pm, Sat 12 pm–6 pm, Closed Sun
CC: A, M, V

Staara designs clothes for professional entertainers, and she also has a custom dressmaking business with a general clientele. If you have a special piece of jewelry and want to dress around it, Staara will design, especially for you, a suit, dress or evening gown at a price starting at $250. Staara and her partner Leda Indio have a selection of unusual contemporary fabrics to choose from, or you can bring in your own fabric. On the floor are ready-made dresses that start at $125; sizes are 8, 10 and 12. Staara designs for female illusionists (female impersonators) and the cross-dressing community (transvestites) so she carries a large selection of lingerie from sizes 34 to 50, and hosiery which will fit the large woman. She also has a private line of heavy duty makeup. This is anything but a run-of-the-mill boutique, and you really ought to pay a visit here. –MC

STATE STREET COLLECTION

609 N State / 60610   951-1828
Hours: Mon 3 pm–6 pm, Tues–Sat 11 am–6 pm, Closed Sun
CC: M, V

You'll swear you just walked into Grandmother's kitchen when you enter this store filled with Art Deco home furnishings, '30s and '40s jewelry and, most important, Depression glassware and kitchenware. The owners, Sandy Johnson and Joan Bartole, both schoolteachers as well as merchants, have created a relaxed, nostalgic atmosphere where you can happily browse, and everything is reasonably priced. Satisfied customers keep coming back for more because everything in the Collection is useful as well as attractive. For example, you'll find '30s telephones as well as vintage clothing among the unusual collectibles. –AT

STUDIO V

672 N Dearborn / 60610   440-1937
Hours: Mon–Sat, 12 pm–6 pm, Sun 1 pm–5 pm (Labor Day to New Year's) Other Suns by chance
CC: A, M, V

Jack Garber loves everything Art Deco. He offers a

wide selection of original objects and quality reproductions of the period from the early '20s through the
arly '50s. You can find jewelry, clothing, lamps, some
kitchenware and books at his neatly packed store in
the River North district. Jack knows his stock very
well, and is active in the collectors' community. He is
one of the founding members of the Chicago Art
Deco Society, which publishes a newsletter and spon-
sors events like Deco balls. He also publishes a list of
vintage stores in the city. He is dedicated to keeping
the current interest in this style alive in Chicago.

The atmosphere of Studio V is perfect, from the
musical standards playing in the background to the
remarkable collection of graphics and posters on sale
on the walls and elsewhere. You can take some of the
atmosphere home with you in various forms: one is a
refurbished telephone, which Jack sells from $50—for
a simple European model—to $300 for more elabo-
rate styles, some with chrome bands and original
cords. These phones are ready to use in any modern
wall jack. Also, Jack has had a large shipment of Fi-
esta ware, in black, pink and grey, and a collection of
whiskey flasks. You can sort through lamps and kitchenware and some beautiful reproductions from a California company: a black amethyst vase with delicate
etchings ($375) and a magnificent lamp with a Tif-
fany feeling ($750). These pieces are all limited edi-
tions. Other handsome reproductions were cubist-
style French lamps ($25 to $300) which go well with
the high tech look, which Jack says resulted from the
Deco craze.

One good reason to go to Studio V is to buy jewelry. The selection is phenomenal. There are cases of
earrings organized by color; hundreds of old pieces

and reproductions. The huge selection of plastics from the '20s and '30s range in price from $5 to $125. The collection of rhinestone pieces was the largest we had seen anywhere with every imaginable color available. And there are compacts, lighters, and cigarette cases.

The clothes, both men's and women's, date mostly from 1915 to 1955. Especially notable were women's '40s suits and older bridal dresses and ball gowns. There were men's vests, jackets, and tuxedos—all in good condition, all reasonably priced, and suits and overcoats. There were new clothes, too, with a vintage feeling: rayon and cotton Hawaiian shirts and flouncy skirts. Bow ties and neckties hang on a rack and there is a tree filled with fascinating hats.

Another interesting area are the bookcases, filled with tongue-in-cheek books, Carmen Miranda paper dolls and Betty Boop memorabilia, among other things. There are also handsome books on Art Deco architecture, greeting cards and posters, all of which make this shop an exciting place for anyone even remotely interested in the period. If you want to join the Chicago Art Deco Society, drop them a line at 823 Lake Street, Oak Park, IL 60301.

So take a trip down memory lane to this wellspring of nostalgia, and plan to stay a while. There's a lot to see. –AT

SUGAR MAGNOLIA

110 E Oak / 60611   944-0885
Hours: Mon–Sat 10 am–6 pm, Sun 12 pm–5 pm (Spring and Summer only)
CC: A, M, V

This attractive boutique always seems to be filled with people plowing through the racks of easy-to-wear, fun clothes. While I was there I saw one woman buying a rhinestone-studded sweatshirt, another looking for a gift for her granddaughter and a young man choosing a shirt and pants. Many of the clothes are unisex. The enthusiastic salesgirls create a kind of dorm-room atmosphere which adds to the shop's appeal.

The shop, which has a new, high-tech look with white tiles and gleaming white fixtures, is filled with eye-catching light-hearted garments from the U.S. and Europe which can easily be mixed and matched, and accessorized to create different looks.

I found a bleached linen jumper which could be worn loose over a bathing suit at the beach, or worn with belt and heels for an evening on the town. Then there was a form-fitting dress in a melon shade of cotton jersey etched with a delicate pattern, for $92. Pants from that same company were $28 and there had been a matching jacket to fling on over it all, but that was sold out. That's a common occurrence at this bustling shop, so be warned—if you see something you like, better not hesitate. It will probably not be there tomorrow.

Owners Jeff and Leslie Gerston also carry some novelties which they design themselves, like Sugar Magnolia T-shirts and sweatshirts. The sweatshirt, at $26, is imprinted with the lyrics of the Grateful Dead song from which the store took its name, and also comes studded with rhinestones for $46. The designs of these shirts change often, so the ones described here might not be in stock by the time you read this.

There is an enormous selection of jewelry, from expensive necklaces and bracelets made of rubber to what Leslie calls "French dimestore stuff"—dozens of varieties of rhinestone jewelry. Prices range from $16 to $100. Sugar Magnolia jewelry looks terrific with the shop's smart clothes.

There are comfortable cotton baby clothes here too, many of them handmade, and many from the same companies which produce the women's things. You might also want to browse a little in the greeting card section of the shop for interesting items.

This enterprising couple travels a great deal, always on the prowl for well-made clothes that look good on different body shapes. Each season they start from scratch, researching the market to find the best because they want to carry only what's right for their store. Everything I saw was right, and I took some of it home with me! –AT

THIS LITTLE PIGGY

Water Tower Place: 835 N Michigan / 60611
943-7449
Hours: Mon & Thurs 10 am–7 pm, Tues, Wed, Fri, Sat
10 am–6 pm, Sun 12 pm–5 pm
CC: A, M, V—$15 minimum

This anklet-sized shop is crammed with the basics and the kooky and arty of the sock world for men, women, and children. Lines carried include Christian Dior, Anne Klein, Evan Picone and Ralph Lauren. There are socks that are ultra sheer and socks that are nubby; there are socks with polka dots, socks with comic book pages, socks with lace and ribbons, socks with punky slash marks, socks with rhinestones, socks with skyscrapers and socks with "Chicago" written on them in glitter. There are wild paisley ultra-sheer leggings by Gamine for $45 and for the Christmas season there were stockings in handknit gold by Sockbrokers. They carry regular nylon stockings—the kind you wear with garters, too. A visit here will give you a leg up on everybody. –AT

ULTIMO

114 E Oak / 60611   787-0906
Hours: Mon–Sat 9:30 am–6 pm, Closed Sun
CC: A, D, M, V

"What do you mean, you can't pronounce it, Dollface! It's ULTIMO! Like ultimate! Like intimate!" So goes a bright new ad in national fashion magazines promoting the New Room at this elegant Gold Coast boutique, where you can buy trendy, moderately-priced clothes with the Ultimo label, and from such lines as Norma Kamali and Willie Wear. You can get a rhinestone-studded T-shirt for $30, and a green and black wool Buffalo jacket for $85. Nothing in the New Room costs more than $330.

Celebrities from everywhere, along with well-dressed locals, trek regularly to this fashion kingdom, which is decorated with cinnabar lacquer, Oriental rugs and Indian printed fabrics, in order to choose from 20 lines by international designers, for both men and women. Owner Joan Weinstein and her assistants search constantly for new, unusual designing talents to keep Ultimo abreast of New York, while bearing in mind the slightly more conservative tastes of Chicago shoppers. I visited Ultimo at the end of the Fall season, and found the exotic: pleated silk shifts and beaded flapper dresses ($2,500), and the practical: black gabardine pants ($250) and casual wear by Donna Karan in plaids and earth tones. A Karan sports jacket was $450. There was a simple, school-girlish Italian wool plaid dress ($800) and a Sonia Rykell velour sweatshirt ($95). And lots of accessories: alligator handbags, oodles of brilliant silk scarves, new way-out rhinestone jewelry from Italy, and belts, hats, gloves and pantyhose.

Lying on a cushion were silk tulle shawls, woven with iridescent threads, sequins, beads, and even garnets. These were numbered and signed by the Japanese designer Kazuko Oshimi, who calls them "poems" ($500 to $1350), and they did indeed look like jeweled sea foam.

John Johnson, the men's buyer, purchases European clothes only, because, he says, American workmanship in men's clothes is not up to Ultimo standards. There were Armani Couture suits ($800) and Missioni sweaters, featured in the Museum of Modern Art in New York ($300 to $500). I saw a rhinestone-studded denim jacket and a buttersoft rayon shirt printed with pictures of New York and Paris, both from Genius, a French sportswear line ($100). The work by Japanese designers has a fuller, softer look than most men's clothing.

If you feel intimidated by Ultimo's prices, remember that the New Room offers reasonable prices, that there are two season-end sales, and that the setting and attitude of the assistants is warm and cozy. You will enjoy a trip to Ultimo. –JJ

THE YESHE COLLECTION

810 W Armitage / 60614   929-6363

Hours: Tues–Sat 12 pm–6 pm, Sun 12 pm–5 pm, Hours flexible
CC: A, M, V

You can spend anything from a few dollars to $750 at this treasure trove of one-of-a-kind textiles, clothing and art objects, many of which are antiques. Phyllis Rosner, the owner, selects the stock during her annual trips to India and the Far East. The average sale here runs around $35, which is really surprising when you consider the rare and unusual things to be found here. Of course if you want a collector's item, you can spend $600 for a hundred-year-old Japanese pillow book consisting of 6 erotic wood block prints. But that is an exception rather than a rule. I found paper garlands from China which would make cheery party decorations, for $4.75, while hanging over Phyllis's antique desk was a brilliantly colored canopy from India ($350); it complemented the delicate old Japanese fans displayed nearby.

There were masks from Argentina and Japan, and a shelf of Russian, Indian and Thai dolls so enchanting that I broke down and bought a lovely, porcelain-headed one from Thailand for $20. If you like to do things in a big way, a life-size soft-sculpture doll can be made to order from a photograph by a company called Out of Our Hands. If you like dolls, this shop is paradise. Phyllis worked as a wholesaler of old Japanese dolls and kimonos before she opened her shop two years ago. And the kimono collection is varied and colorful. You wouldn't want to throw one on after a shower, of course. They are intended for luxurious lounging and evening wear or for some special occasion. There are long and short ones, lined and unlined, for $65 to $500. On the wall was a white silk wedding dress embroidered with peacocks. Phyllis always has traditional Oriental fabrics, as well as pillows and small purses made from old obis and the cuffs of opera robes.

Then there is the handmade jewelry. When I was there Phyllis was unpacking a box of old Naga necklaces, all in very good condition. The many strands of extremely small colored beads which create the special look of a Naga necklace cost from $200 to $400. You won't see duplicates of Phyllis's earrings—some beaded, many silver and brass—anywhere in the city. Also you can find beads here from all over the world, from which you can create your own necklace. Prices vary from 45¢ for little onyx beads to $10 for large amber balls. Occasionally Phyllis offers jewelry-making classes. Inquire if you're interested.

All in all, a visit to this Collection with its array of textures and colors is a spell-binding experience. -AT

ALL OUR CHILDREN

2217 N Halsted / 60614   327-1868
Hours: Tues, Wed, Fri 10 am–6 pm, Thurs 10 am–7
pm, Sat 10 am–5 pm, Sun 12 pm–5 pm, Closed Mon
CC: A, M, V

This shop, in the Halsted-Sheffield area which is quickly filling with interesting boutiques, carries better-quality children's and infant's wear up to size 7, both American and European, many in natural fibers. The sales staff are experienced in child-rearing and offer assistance with a smile, whether customers are seeking clothes, accessories or shower gifts. I especially admired the pajamas and little robes. The specialty here is unusual garments. A nifty play area is provided, so feel free to bring the little ones along for the ride –AT

ANASTASIA

2621 N Halsted / 60614   281-1800
Hours: Tues–Fri 12 pm–7 pm, Sat 12 pm–6 pm, Sun 12
pm–5 pm, Closed Mon
CC: A, M, V

This jazzy boutique specializes in fascinating fun clothing and jewelry. Owner Nancy Stanley goes to France and Italy to bring back clothing with a European flair. A unique, trendy, handmade imported outfit is yours at an average price of $150. There are blown glass earrings for $20 and gigantic rhinestone ones for $60, and other imported costume jewelry made of wood, bone, pearl and other interesting materials. Some have an elegant Bulgari look without

Bulgari prices. Anastasia has light-weight wool coats:
one, for spring, wraps around the neck and drapes to
mid-calf. It is available in white, red and black, in
sizes small, medium and large, and sells for $194.
There are casual clothes here, in cotton in summer
and in light wool in the fall: oversized tops, pants and
skirts with elastic waists, so although Anastasia's sizes
go from very small to 12 or 14, many of these outfits
will fit larger women. There are belts and scarves too,
and unusual leather jackets at $195 in purple, loden
green and black, all in small, medium and large.
Merchandise turns over rapidly here, so if you're interested, don't hesitate! –MC

APROPOS

3315 N Broadway / 60657   528-2130
Hours: Mon–Fri. 11 am–7 pm Winter, 12 pm–8 pm
Summer, Sat 11 am–6 pm, Sun 12 pm–5 pm
CC: A, M, V

This delightful women's clothing boutique is filled
to the brim with things that are oh, so appropriate!
The prices are moderate to high, and the fashions are
quality—just right. There are both dressy and sporty
clothes, mostly separates, with a few dresses; there are
cotton jumpsuits in one-size-fits-all, the Cut Loose
Line of cotton knits in bright pastels that are pre-dyed
and pre-shrunk, New Hero American cotton dresses,
pants, skirts and cruisewear and, in the winter, sleep-
wear for women and children. If you're in the market
for legwear, Apropos has a great selection of socks and
pantyhose ranging from the understated to the out-
right funky. There is some lingerie and a lot of jewelry, ranging from replicas of Victorian antiques to

big rhinestone pieces and big earrings at prices from $12 to $40 or $50. The cotton components for exercise and sport are sold all the year 'round. And at Christmas don't forget that Apropos carries stuffed animals. –AT

BALLOONS TO YOU

3225 N Sheffield / 60657   327-0909
Hours: Mon–Fri 9 am–6 pm, Sat 10 am–5 pm, Closed Sun
CC: A, M, V

If you're having a party—whether it's a bar mitzvah, a birthday, or a wedding—Nancy Rieff has loads of party paraphernalia and services to save time for you and provide fun for your guests. If you want a singing clown or a fanciful red rooster to deliver balloons and entertain your guests, Nancy will arrange it for between $35 and $50. For weddings and bar mitzvahs—and whatever else you want—Nancy will design a special balloon centerpiece just for you. Balloons To You is also a retail store, selling cards, candles, balloons, puzzles and silk-screened T-shirts and sweatshirts. –MC

THE BAOBAB TREE

3635 N Broadway / 60613   935-9114
Hours: Mon–Fri 6 pm–9 pm, Sat & Sun 11 am–6 pm, or by appt
CC: M, V

The specialty here is African artifacts and clothing. Thick wool rugs in earth tones run from $40 for a

2' × 4' to $300 for a 9' × 6'. Larger sizes can be specially ordered. A traditional Zulu grain basket is $70; smaller straw baskets run $5 to $10. Pillow covers and shawls in soft pastel mohair are $25 to $35; mohair wall hangings depicting village scenes have to be seen to be appreciated: their colors are extremely lustrous because they are done from vegetable dyes. They cost from $50 up. While you are in this pleasant lower-level shop, run by Martin Whitefield and Aaron Byrd, take a look at the white cotton unisex shirts. They are hand-embroidered and you can take one home for around $30. –MC

BENETTON'S

2828 N Clark (Century Mall) / 60657   972-7111
(See listing under Near North)

BLAKE

2448 N Lincoln / 60614   477-3364
Hours: Mon–Sat 11 am–8 pm, Sun 12 pm–5 pm
CC: A, M, V

This is a store with an individual stamp, offering women's and unisex clothing which is up-to-the-minute and very comfortable. The engaging owners, Dominic Marchesi and Marilyn Blaszka, who met originally when they were both students at the Art Institute's junior school, hunt everywhere—including England—to bring Chicago the best selection they can find of reasonably priced fashion-forward merchandise. This shop, which they opened in 1984, is designed to showcase clothes against a simple, uncluttered background. The day I was there the customers were a varied group—young and old, business women and male models, city folk and suburbanites—all drawn by clothes in the forefront of fashion, from street wear to the ultra casual and relaxed.

I saw a line by Katherine Hamnett, an English designer who has become extremely famous. Then there is English Eccentrics, a line designed by three women, which adds a twist to classic silk shirts. They are done in a bold print and the sleeves are extra-long so that they can be rolled up. They are unisex and sell for an average of around $100. I bought a white cotton ribbed oversized dress made by an American company called Tornado. At $70 it was a typical Tornado body-conscious garment. Blake carries also a similar line called Leon Max. Another line the people at Blake like is Go-. There are washable silk separates for men and women: shirts, skirts, pants, jackets and tops in a range of $120 to $160.

In the spring you will find cotton sweaters here, usually with bold patterns, and in winter a selection of quiet wool sweaters ranging from $60 to $200. Blake sees the newest look as a narrower silhouette for men and women—not so full as garments have been.

The day I was there, I saw a nice selection of accessories—rhinestone earrings and necklaces, hats, leather belts and socks by Hue. A visit to Blake is a really exhilarating experience. –AT

BOOMERANG

3352 N Halsted / 60657   348-7755
Hours: Tues–Fri 1 pm–7 pm, Sat 12 pm–7 pm, Sun 1 pm–5 pm, Closed Mon
CC: M, V

David Pinson and Randy Nixon, who have collected '50s furniture and accessories for as long as they can remember, opened Boomerang in 1983 to sell '40s and '50s furniture by famous American and European designers, along with jewelry and accessories for the home. This is the only store in the Midwest that sells what has been called "Mid-century Modern," and the prices are about half what they would be in New York. I sat in a comfortable lounge chair designed by Charles Eames in the '40s. Its price was $400, it is made of moulded plywood, and it is a good example of this shop's practical and aesthetically pleasing collection. There is decorative art also—enamels, sculpture—and sometimes china and flatware of the period, and rugs. For between $45 to $300 you can buy Mexican and American silver jewelry—earrings, bracelets, necklaces, belt buckles—and there are floor and ceiling lamps and moulded plastic European lighting. There are novelty items as well, and TVs and radios. Boomerang helped to outfit Ed Debevic's restaurant. –AT

CHICAGO COSTUME COMPANY

1120 W Fullerton / 60614   528-1264
Hours: Mon–Wed 9 am–5 pm, Thurs, Fri 9 am–7 pm,
Sat 10 am–6 pm, Sun 12 pm–6 pm
CC: A, M, V, Disc

Whatever the occasion—Halloween, Masquerade Ball, Christmas—you can outfit yourself here. Owner Mary Hickey's main business is selling and renting costumes to local theatres and TV stations; at this store she caters to the public, both selling and renting costumes. Expensive, handmade costumes are rented at an average fee of $35 to $125 for three days. These are costumes like the Cabbage Patch Doll ($90 rental) and the Mae West ensemble ($100 rental). Less expensive costumes are sold: the Nun costume costs $30, the Pirate $25, the Witch $32 and the Devil Man or Woman $35. The range of costumes sold is $20 to $90. Latex masks—Dracula, Medusa, Cyclops, etc.—are sold for $25 to $60. There are hats, too: British Constable for $9, a Pirate hat for $14. Then there is theatrical makeup in many colors, to apply yourself at home, by Bob Kelly, Bennye and Zauder. At the moment, according to Mary, the popular new costume look is the inanimate object. For $55 you can be an orange, carrot, tomato, apple, chocolate chip cookie, watermelon, porkchop or slice of bread. A refundable security deposit is required for rentals. Mary suggests that you come here for gifts for the hard to shop for. –MC

CLARK STREET WALTZ

2360 N Lincoln / 60614   472-5559
Hours: Tues–Sat 1 pm–6 pm, Sun 1 pm–5 pm, Closed Mon
CC: A, M, V

This six-year-old store specializes in all things old and beautiful: Japanese silk kimonos, white Victorian petticoats and gowns and a fine selection of vintage dresses and blouses. But Clark Street Waltz also carries new accessories: hats, derbys, straw hats, scarves, gloves, pants and skirts in sizes petite to extra-large. There is new jewelry of all kinds, and especially silver rings and earrings hand-made just for this shop by a New Hampshire silversmith. Silk embroidered shawls decorate the walls to recreate—along with wicker furniture, high tin ceilings and Oriental rugs—the best of bygone days. Be sure and check out all the old glassware, the rhinestone jewelry and the 1940s blouses, all of which sell for under $16.00. –AT

DÉGAGÉ

2246 N Clark / 60614   935-7737
Hours: Mon–Fri 10 am–7 pm, Sat 10 am–6 pm, Sun 12 pm–5 pm
CC: M, V

In the winter this shop carries a fairly conservative stock, with women's suits by Ellen Tracy, along with quality contemporary sportswear. But in summer owner Bonnie Paul lets loose and brings in trendier garments from here and abroad and lots of novelty jewelry done by designers from New York and Paris. In winter you can find hand-knit sweaters in the $125-$250 range; there are always scarves and belts and stirrup pants and oversized shirts. Sizes are 4 to 12. Women drive all the way from Highland Park to shop here—that certainly says something for the appeal of the fashions in Dégagé's new, bigger location next door to the old one. Drop in and don't forget to check out the French fashion pantyhose and novelty socks while you're here. –AT

DEI GIOVANI

2421 N Clark / 60614   549-4116
(See listing under Near North)

DIVINE IDEA

2863 N Clark / 60657   975-0909
Hours: Mon–Sat 11 am–7 pm, Sun 12 pm–6 pm
CC: M, V

Whether you're going to a costume party, a concert by the latest hot punk group, or just looking for something different to spice up a dull closet, and you don't want to spend a lot of money, then you'll find these vintage, and new, fashions for men and women to be just the ticket. There are a large variety of clothing and accessories at very reasonable prices, and in a great setting. Saturday afternoon here is as much fun as any party—people walking around in amazing get-ups, complete strangers helping one another put together whole looks in a matter of minutes in this, the third home for Divine Idea since 1979, and the largest, with spacious dressing-rooms, racks and racks of fashions from the '40s through the '60s, and occasionally some handmade clothes by local designers at fairly high prices.

David Berg runs the shop, which was actually the brainstorm of Joette Waters, his wife, who was an inveterate scavenger, but who turned the shop over to David because she and two friends star in a vocal group called Stardust. The group specializes in songs from the '30s, '40s and '50s. Their gowns are all courtesy of Divine Idea, although many of their hats are by Raymond Hudd. Stardust is as much fun to watch as to listen to, and you can get their performance schedule at this store.

There is a wonderful collection of cocktail and day dresses, few evening dresses ($8 to $30), and a definitive selection of Hawaiian and bowling shirts: Hawaiian shirts are $12, men's bowling shirts are $9, women's $14 (never-worn). I saw some with interesting details—like buttons etched with bowling pins. There are always hundreds of crisp tuxedo shirts, mostly from the '60s, for $10 and $12. And how about a yellow satin formal bow tie ($6) and matching cummerbund ($10)? In the winter you will find a lot of military gear from the U.S. and Europe. Sports coats and hundreds of skinny ties ($6) are displayed under old posters. There is an entire section for '60s clothes.

Some of the new clothes include hand-painted T-shirts, stirrup pants, lace stretch pants and accessories like sunglasses. But new things are coming in all the time here. Some of the jewelry is new, and some is vintage. One real bargain is robes which are unisex and made of shiny rayon at $18 and $22, and cotton kimonos at $20. Another great buy is men's vintage overcoats, which are also worn by women, and never-worn men's suits and jackets from the '50s and '60s which can also be made over to fit women. (See Studio Sew Sew entry). Finally, there are fedoras aplenty here, along with *24,000 pairs* of brushed nylon gloves from the '60s in varying lengths and just about every color. So everyone can find something here to love.
–AT

ELLE BOUTIQUE

3405 N Broadway / 60657   327-2145
Hours: Mon–Sat 11 am–7 pm, Sun 12 pm–5 pm
CC: A, M, V, Disc

In this elegant shop French pop music plays over the speakers, and the walls are covered with bevelled mirrors from the ceiling to within a few inches of the floor, where Oriental rugs cover the dark gray carpeting. Michele Kane, a Frenchwoman who was an assistant buyer at Henri Bendel, has, with permission, modeled her store after the Elle Boutique in Paris. If all this sounds expensive—it is. Many of Michele's lines are her exclusive imports; there are usually no more than six or seven of each garment. But the atmosphere is not intimidating, and both Michele and her French assistants are eager to make you feel welcome.

The leather clothes here are French and Italian imports and the leather is soft as butter. One oversized jacket-and-stirrup-pants in deep purple suede and leather went for $650; as did a caramel-colored leather bolero jacket and matching stirrups by Singulier, a French company carried exclusively in this country by Michele. There are beautiful mohair and wool coats designed by Marie Beltramie, in warm colors: I loved one gigantic one in deep blue with a soft velvet shawl color, and, instead of buttons, arrow-shaped flaps which fit cleverly inside the waistband ($625). Winter clothes here cost much more than summer clothes because of higher priced winter materials.

Claude Bert's suits (one classic black suit had an elongated tux jacket with a satin collar and satin stripes down the sides of both the jacket and the slim knee-length skirt) run about $375, but the summer styles (white cotton pleated pants and matching military jacket) are about $175 for the set. European silks Michele finds too expensive to import at all: she has a good selection of silk shirts from a domestic company called Stefano Studio. I liked a flirty short-sleeved blouse with shoulder pads, available in solid yellow, black or fuschia ($68) and matching skirt ($49). *And* unusual accessories: a white leather belt with dangling crystal and silver pieces ($95) and a clear plastic belt with pink hearts down its length ($65). And plainer alligator and supple leather belts from France and Italy.

Finally, there is the jewelry: a cord necklace of Italian leather hung with large silver disks and shells was $105, a typical price for necklaces here. Hats, made by an 80-year-old German whose company is called Chapeau Creations, are somewhat costly at $80. But they supply hats for *Dynasty* too, so watch for them on TV. All in all, Elle is a happy addition to the city. –AT

ERINISLE

2246 N Clark / 60614   975-6616
Hours: Mon–Fri 11 am–7 pm, Sat 10 am–6 pm, Sun 12 pm–5 pm, Closed Mon, Memorial Day to Labor Day
CC: M, V

If you want unusual quality clothing for men and women and/or a well-made gift, there are many shops you can visit—but if, in addition, you want these things to be imported from Ireland, go to Erinisle, which Mary Dugan opened in 1976. After you have lunch in one of the many nearby restaurants, stop by and browse in a relaxed Irish atmosphere. There are the traditional cable-knit sweaters and tweeds ($49 to $500), offered year round; tweed and wool coats in both men's and women's sizes run from $250 to $400. In summer there are linen clothes and cotton sweaters which start at $65. There are neckties, scarves, gloves and hats—unisex—,throws and shawls. And unusual pottery and glassware, which would be perfect as wedding gifts. Prices are reasonable if you take the shop's high standards into consideration, and the meticulous attention that has been paid to details. –AT

FLASHY TRASH

3521 N Halsted / 60657   327-6900
Hours: Mon–Sat 12 pm–7 pm, Sun 12 pm–6 pm
CC: A, M, V

Here's the place to get a complete vintage wardrobe. Harold Mandell's motto is "from Camp to Classics." The selection is almost overwhelming. There are two rooms of evening wear, one for men and one for women, and the evening wear is sumptuous. There are velvet opera cloaks, some lined with ermine or encrusted with beads ($200), racks of '40s and '50s cocktail and ball gowns for between $18 and $85. For men there are handsome tuxedos—many never worn—from the 1890s through the 1960s. A complete suit, including a crisp white tuxedo shirt, will set you back about $75. Harold has a vast number of sources to buy from, both here and in England. He is well-known because he supplies period clothing and accessories to TV stations and to advertising agencies for magazines ads.

He stocks a lot of never-worn clothing: a big supply of coats and overcoats, for instance, and vintage shoes from the '30s to the '60s for both men and women. And there is lingerie. The selections are vast: silk and satin nightgowns, teddies, bed jackets and never-worn slips for her; upper-class smoking jackets and robes for him—including a silk Lanvin robe for $60. Half the stock is everyday clothes. Especially worth noting are never-worn men's swim trunks and a huge collection of women's blouses—solid and print, short sleeves and long—for $15. And there is legwear, a specialty here. Striped, spotted, zebra pantyhose ($8.50), fishnets in all colors ($7) and socks! Lace neon slouch socks ($10), over-the-knee styles ($12) crinkled anklets ($6.50) and men's never-worn socks from the '40s and '50s, most still carrying the original price tag ($10). Also never-worn are bow ties ($5), some with matching cummerbunds and narrow neckties from the early '60s ($6 to $8). Behind the counter Harold stores suspenders, both new and old, in checks, zebra stripes and solids. And gloves here run the gamut from fingerless gauntlets ($6) to opera-length mauve doeskin ($40).

There are eight showcases of jewelry here, running the gamut from Victorian to '50s glass and sterling. A speciality is men's Art Deco watches which start at $125.

I almost forgot to mention top hats and derbies, which are bought by both men and women, and Art Deco pottery and other gift items, like boxes and picture frames. In addition, Harold experiments from time to time with new designers, whose work he shows for trial periods that change seasonally. Everyone from bag ladies to Prince shops at Flashy Trash, so give yourself a treat and drop in! –AT

GIUSEPPI

2050 N Halsted / 60614   525-6311
Hours: Mon–Fri 12 pm–7 pm, Sat 11 am–6 pm, Sun 12 pm–5 pm
CC: A, M, V

This is a men's shop with colorful clothes in up-to-the-minute styles. Owner Joe Gagliano says that his shop is a center of energy for clothing, and his goods are indeed lively and exciting, and his prices reasonable. Everything here is casual, and over half the clothing is unisex and can be—and is—bought by women. Cotton T-shirts go for $12.50, surfing jams and cotton sweaters for $30 and $50. In the summer Joe sells tons of cotton clothing; in the winter he concentrates on cruisewear—a great idea, because it's difficult to find lightweight men's wear in Chicago in the winter. He has wool sweaters in bright colors with geometric designs ($50) and corduroy pants and blue jeans. So come to this friendly shop for easy-going, comfortable dressing, be you male or female. –MC

GLORIA

1007 W Webster / 60614   327-9665
Hours: Mon–Sat 1 pm–7 pm, Sun–by chance
CC: A, M, V

This vintage shop is like a lively museum; it can take quite a while for a browser to see everything. The very large room is divided into sections for furs, coats, dresses, jewelry, lingerie, shoes, men's clothing and old radios, TV sets and various ornaments. The look is neat and attractive—like the owner, Gloria McCartney, who for ten years was a partner in a successful vintage store called Kitsch, and who has been collecting vintage clothing for 20 years.

Gloria's furs are stashed toward the rear of the shop. They are quality furs in perfect condition. I loved a full-length red fitch coat which was priced $400. There were a few opera coats with velvet collars for between $100 and $200. In the dress section were silk evening dresses—some with embroidery—but they weren't cheap. A pre-World War I pink gown was $250 and a beaded pale green silk blouse from the '20s was going for $300. Lingerie is expensive too. But prices for shoes—and Gloria has a terrific collection of high-heeled pumps—range from $15 to $45.

In jewelry for vintage lovers there are plenty of rhinestone pieces; but there are also some striking earrings by Chicago designers. And there are restored men's watches from the '40s selling for $100–$150. And cuff links and tie clips are of varying quality and price.

There is a big selection of men's clothing. Shirts from the '40s and '50s, carrying the Bob Hope and Perry Como labels, sell for $85 to $125. Suits and sport coats start at $40, and Tuxedos in perfect condition run $75 to $125. Ties go for $8 to $10.

You can pick up an old radio or a black and white TV set here in working condition. And there are display cases filled with Russell Wright pottery, and with reptile handbags—Gloria has loads of them. A red lizard bag will set you back from $35 to $75.

Gloria also designs and knits her own sweaters. These are really beautiful, but they run from $150 to $600. And she has unisex clothes.

It's obvious that you won't find any bargains at Gloria's. However, each month on the night of the full moon, Gloria discounts everything 20% to 50%. She serves wine and stays open until midnight. If you can't work out the dates, watch for the *Reader* ad or call her and she will put you on her mailing list. –MC

GOODIES

3450 N Halsted / 60657   477-8223
Hours: Wed–Sat 12 pm–7 pm, Sun 12 pm–6 pm, Closed
Mon & Tues
CC: Cash Or Check Only

Ted Frankel describes his store as " a vintage fun house" and, incredibly, one dollar will buy you many of the old-fashioned toys and other things which are displayed on the shelves or tossed apparently haphazardly into baskets. Ten dollars can practically buy you the world here. There are wind-up and battery-operated vintage toys, large cigar labels, old movie star items, and kitschy things like toasters and salt-and-pepper shakers and harmonicas from occupied Japan. There are gyroscopes and Slinkies and unique children's books, most of them pop-up books or other interesting kinds. And there is lots of jewelry. Ted buys out old costume jewelry warehouses, so he has all kinds of jewelry from the '40s, '50s and '60s. He has, for instance, sterling silver finger rings for $2. Seventy-five percent of his stock is old, and about 25% is new. So drop into Goodies, where all sorts of collectibles and amusing items will surprise and delight you, and your pocketbook won't suffer. –AT

I.K. DON

3174 N Clark / 60657   549-4449
Hours: Mon–Fri 12 pm–9 pm, Sat 10:30 am–8 pm, Sun
12 pm–6 pm
CC: A, M, V

This shop features trendy sportswear, both men's and "unisex." There are jeans imported from Japan and Italy, among other places. It's difficult to pin down the price range because of the wide variety of manufacturers represented here, but Izzy says you can spend from $5 to $500 at his shop. You'll find lines here that aren't at the bigger stores, such as Shanghai Sportswear, New Man and GB Clothing, among others, and all items are unique. Top coats, trousers, sports jackets, and sweaters are here in "with-it" abundance. –AT

INDULGENCE

2625 N Clark / 60614   281-9009
Hours: Tues, Wed, Sat, Sun 11 am–7 pm, Thurs & Fri
11 am–8 pm
CC: A, M, V, Disc

This women's boutique offers clothes in a simplified range of colors: black, white, red or gray—urban colors, displayed in a setting designed to look like an urban back yard. The walls are painted with fences and doors, and the clothing is showcased on cement blocks. A somewhat odd section filled with feather boas, fans and masks made sense to me when I learned that Mary Hickey who owns the Chicago Costume Company, also owns this relatively new shop. Mary has designed a line of evening clothes: I liked one in black and red with an organdy ruffle and satin trim. Prices for the gowns run between $100 and $300. The feather boas, which come from turkeys and ostriches, run $35 to $75. In addition to these things, Indulgence carries shiny spandex unisex pants, dressy hats, leather and rubber handbags ($10 to $125), socks, lace tights and lace body suits and gold tinsel wigs. The clothes are the clothes you see in *Mademoiselle* and *Elle* magazines. Then there is the jewelry. There are Melody Fenton's designs of new wave pins and earrings for Bijou Graphics ($10 to $30) and Marcia Brenner's Just Jewelry—a line of crystal earrings running $5 to $50. Linda Marie's Indulge line of earrings are made exclusively for Indulgence. And don't forget to look at the lamé gloves.

Every night you can see people at Limelight, George's and The Riviera dressed in clothes from Indulgence. Most of the garments will not work at the office, but the World's Apart line of brushed cotton separates will look great anywhere, day or night. –AT

JÂCHER

2419 N Clark / 60614   327-7711
Hours: Mon–Fri 11 am–7 pm, Sat 10:30 am–5:30 pm,
Sun 12 pm–4 pm
CC: A, M, V

You will find casual clothes for women here, most designed by Chicagoans, including students at the Art Institute, and also by lesser-known designers from all over the country. These clothes are not sold at department stores. Many of them are one-size-fits-all, and there are lots of loose-fitting dresses, so Jâcher is a perfect place for heavy women to shop. Owners Cheryl Segal and Arlene Minkus, who opened the store in 1980, have won the hearts of customers by placing special orders for sizes and colors. Prices are moderate. In the winter you will find unique handmade sweaters in the $80 to $250 range, and a lot of handpainted shirts, sweatshirts and dresses. Pants, some with elastic waists, run petite, small, medium and large, and there are two-piece pants and top outfits. In the $60 to $400 range, there are suede and leather dresses, pants, tunic and tops by Mongé, a Chicago designer. There are belts and scarves and a good selection of jewelry: ceramic, enamelled, rhinestone, brass, copper, nickel earrings and necklaces in a price range from $18 to $120. –AT

LA COQUETTE

2858 N Clark / 60657   248-3905
Hours: Tues–Fri 10:30 am–7:30 pm, Sat 10:30 am–
6 pm, Sun 12 pm–5 pm, Closed Mon
CC: A, M, V

This pretty little shop is filled with lingerie, foundations and loungewear, most of it handpainted, handmade and manufactured in Chicago by Hyun. Owner Mary Bartels, it is obvious, likes bright colors. I bought an unusual emerald green charmeuse camisole and tap pant for $88. Shiny charmeuse (silk fabric) nightgowns in bright and pastel colors are about $125, filmy handpainted silk chiffon robes are $195 and well-made purple teddies with black lace trim are $78. La Coquette carried stockings as well as pantyhose and garter belts, not always easy to find. All sizes are stocked. In one antique display case I saw silk flower petal earrings for the boudoir. At $14 they would make an unusual and lovely gift. –MC

LATHAM LIMITED

509 W Diversey Pkwy / 60614   248-3464
1133 N State / 60610   787-9349

540 N Michigan / 60611   644-0323
Hours: State St & Michigan Ave Mon–Fri 10:30 am–
6:30 pm, Sat 10 am–6 pm. Diversey Pkwy Mon & Thurs
11:30 am–7:30 pm, Tues, Wed, Fri 10:30 am–6:30 pm,
Sat 10 am–6 pm
CC: A, C, D, M, V

Joann and Bernard Latham enjoy performing what they consider an essential service for today's working woman. The managers of their stores are experienced saleswomen who keep lists of each customer's purchases and notes on the kind of clothes that customer is looking for. The sales staff can coordinate your wardrobe for you. The Latham stores carry business clothes and sportswear by Perry Ellis, Calvin Klein, Ellen Tracy and Liz Claiborne. Clothes come in sizes 4 to 14. During the winter months you can find a good selection of resort wear at this interesting little chain, which also carries accessories, including belts, pantyhose and coordinating separates. –MC

LES PRIMITIFS

2038 N Clark / 60614   528-5200
Hours: Tues–Fri 12 pm–7 pm, Sat & Sun 12 pm–6 pm,
Closed Mon
CC: A, M, V

This gallery sells primarily African art objects, but there are things also from New Guinea, Tibet, Indonesia, Afghanistan and Pakistan. The owner, Keithe Barton and his wife Irene, import one-of-a-kind pieces; he travels widely. There is wooden sculpture here from six inch figurines to Kalo birds from the Ivory Coast which go up to five or six feet in height and sell from $200 to $2000. There are masks, musical instruments and puppets, some of which are painted. The masks start at $100. Then there are baskets, pottery and terra cottas in a range from $250 to $800 or $900. There are interesting rectangular wall hangings and Khilim rugs from Afghanistan and Pakistan. The jewelry is unusual and attractive: earrings, beaded necklaces from Bali (around $60), ivory bracelets, African finger rings and some Afghan jewelry. The price range for the jewelry is $10 to $80. –MC

MEXICAN FOLK ARTS

2433 N Clark / 60614   871-1511
Hours: Mon–Fri 11:30 am–7 pm, Sat 10:30 am–6 pm,
Sun 11:30 am–5 pm
CC: A, M, V

This glittering shop with its Saltillo tile floor is packed to the rafters with clothing, jewelry, pottery, and gift items from Mexico and South America. The owners, Eugenia Fawcett and Marcy Milner, opened the shop 13 years ago, and have been going twice a year to Mexico ever since, to choose their imports with care and from a knowledge of Latin America's rich cultural history.

There are ethnic clothes here: wedding-dresses ($100-$200) and hand-embroidered dresses from $38. In the summer you can find men's and women's huaraches with rubber or leather soles, elastic-waisted skirts in attractively colored cottons and some unisex shirts and pants. In the fall and winter the store is piled with sweaters in soft light wools and a variety of colors, and heavy embroidered cardigans ($70 to $90 range). Handsome oversized cotton jackets run $50 to $60.

Winter and summer there are heavy cotton dresses with both long and short sleeves in the $50 range as well as beautiful soft serapes in deep shades of blue and plum wool. Kenya bags in oatmeal and understated colors run about $28.

The jewelry display is impressive: mostly silver, but also gold and brass rings, bracelets, necklaces and earrings, both Mexican and from local designers. And you can buy charming little carved animals for around $12. For under $10 there are woven purses and colorful sashes. And for more expensive gifts there are handblown glasses from Guadalajara and Talavera china from Pueblo. Beautiful pottery is available here too, and hand-made wall-hangings.

While you are there, be sure and notice the beautiful hand-painted chest near the front of the shop. The owners won't want to sell it, but they'll tell you all about how they found it. So spend a pleasant hour in Mexico on Clark Street. –MC

MY OWN TWO FEET

2148 N Halsted / 60614   935-3338
Hours: Tues, Wed, Fri, 10 am–6 pm, Thurs 11 am–7 pm, Sat 10 am–5 pm, Sun 12 pm–5 pm, Closed Mon
CC: A, M, V

This shop specializes in children's shoes and accessories, both imported and domestic. Owners Kim Rome and Debbie Litke are determined to prevent any child from owning their shoes unless they are a perfect fit. They believe also in quality service. There are inexpensive canvas shoes in infant-to-teen sizes. But the imported dress shoes are eye-catching—and expensive. Italian diBrazzi and Zenotti dress shoes in leather and patent leather run between $30 and $75. Kim and Debbie go frequently to Europe to buy. There is also a large selection of socks, anklets and tights. And you can find hundreds of items for birthday gifts for under $10. Try a clever little toy or piece of jewelry. Great idea! –MC

NONPAREIL

2300 N Clark / 60614   477-2933
Hours: Mon–Fri 11 am–7 pm, Sat 10 am–6 pm, Sun 12 pm–5 pm
CC: A, M, V

This is the place for the gift for the person you can never find a gift for. In this delightful shop, flooded with natural light from two floor-to-ceiling windows, you can find everything from bookends made from old trophies painted with acrylics, to women's clothes on the very cutting edge of fashion. The inventory is very large: Marjorie Freed, the creative owner of this 8-year-old business, believes that the more people see, the more they can assimilate. It's difficult to describe the unusual pieces handcrafted by David Kirk— wooden sculpture with moving parts which run from $150 to $300. Then there are Craig and Judy Carey's hand-painted chairs, mirrors, birdhouses—and even an armoire. (One mirror with shelf had painted snakes winding about its edges). Prices of Carey designs run from $30 to $300. There are interesting toys and books for children; even adults buy the Japanese robots. You can spend a good deal of time sorting through the baskets of inexpensive goodies: trays that make ice cubes shaped like elephants, unusual rubber stamps... And there is a fine collection of beautiful Indian and Afghan rugs folded up in a corner.

You will not see yourself coming and going in Nonpareil clothes, which are off-beat without being far out, and which are casual and comfortable. The price range is moderate to expensive, aimed at the 22 to 35 age range. The Vinh Pharm line is here and Jim Ewing/Bis. Clothes are simple, and so are the belts and bags, all updated classics. There are hats, sashes and socks. *And* there is the jewelry. An entire wall is hung with one-of-a-kind necklaces in every conceivable length, style and price range. For $20 I bought an East Indian necklace: a series of satin cords hung with little cupids and bells to frighten demons away. A hip-length string of fake pearls went for $42. The earrings were certainly "non-traditional"—sushi earrings at $18 and other striking designs in natural materials at about $25. And, if you're fed up with digital watches, you can find refurbished vintage watches here, dating from about 1915 to 1955. So stop by and plan to pick up some outstanding gifts for yourself and your friends. –AT

OMIYAGE LTD.

2482 N Lincoln / 60614   477-1428
Hours: Tues-Sat 11 am–6:30 pm, Sun 12 pm–5 pm,
Closed Mon
CC: M, V

A mother-daughter team, Sally Otsuji and Karen Damato, run this gift store which they call a "people's accessories" business. The merchandise—from the antique Japanese wedding robe they once sold, to the wide range of handmade and vintage jewelry or hand-painted T-shirts—is one-of-a-kind for the most part and in the low-to-moderate price range. There are many antiques, but also kitchen items and ceramics designed by artists both local and from outside Chicago. You need to look over the wide range of gifts. –AT

PANACHE HANDBAGS AND ACCESSORIES, INC.

2252 N Clark / 60614   477-4537
Hours: Mon–Fri 10 am–7 pm, Sat 10 am–6 pm, Sun 12 pm–5 pm
CC: M, V

This is a wow of a little place which features accessories any woman might want to bring some zing to an old dress or just to wear with anything. Panache carries handbags, scarves, belts, sunglasses and about 500 lines of jewelry, with taste running to the fashion-forward. Lynn Greenbaum is the energetic proprietor. She buzzes in and out, helping customers to find the right handbag or necklace to tone up any outfit. All the clothes at Panache are designed by Reggie Thomas, a Chicago designer. They are casual, one-size-fits-all in varying colors and fabrics and they flatter everyone. Prices range from $15 to $300 in this store, so you have a good deal of latitude. –AT

PORT OF ENTRY

2032 N Halsted / 60614   348-4550
Hours: Tues–Thurs 12 pm–6:30 pm, Fri 12 pm–8 pm, Sat 10 am–6 pm, Sun 12 pm–6 pm, Closed Mon
CC: A, M, V

This attractive boutique offers fine, stylish and yet

conservative clothing at moderate prices to the professional woman, or to anyone who likes beautiful colors and natural fabrics. You'll also find large women's sizes here (up to 16) as well as one-size-fits-all fashions. Owners Barbara and Ron Schultz opened the shop 8 years ago in an old brownstone which they rehabbed. Ron, a graphic designer, created the up-to-date layout as well as the charming brick-lined garden before the front door.

Barbara, who studied fashion illustration at the Art Institute and the American Academy of Art, does the buying in New York, LA and San Francisco. She carries Sarah Arizona, a line with an easy Santa Fe feeling: Sarah Arizona does two-piece outfits in beautifully colored rayon. Cha Cok, a French artist, designs clothes with a unique look, and West Indian designer Jimmy Walker does exclusive silk screen summer fashions. From New York comes Arlequinne, a line of whimsical separates made of cotton. The Schultzes like to encourage talented new designers and you'll see some one-of-a-kind things here as a result.

There are cotton T-shirts, shells and turtlenecks at reasonable prices, available year 'round. Barbara says these wash well without shrinking, and she should know since almost her entire wardrobe comes from the shop. In winter, you'll find sweaters, handknit in Toronto, which start at $60.

The jewelry, like the clothes, is unique and clean-lined. There are streamlined pins—Deco reproductions—for $30. Some of the bead necklaces, from $100 to $150, are made by Chicago designers. In fact, most of the necklaces, bracelets and earrings are handmade. I loved an award-winning geometric necklace made in burnished metal by a Toronto artist. Most of the jewelry, which has a lot of style, is under $70.

Don't leave the store without looking at the scarf collection. There were cotton scarves from Italy at $45, handpainted silk ones from $24 to $52, and handwoven ones at $24. Both Barbara and her friendly manager Andrea help you to choose accessories—many of them English—for any dress or outfit you buy. The atmosphere is relaxed: women of all shapes and sizes can experiment here with new designs and interesting color combinations.

People come here from the city and the suburbs, from the corporate world and from the world of the arts. You come too. -AT

PRESENCE

2501 N Clark / 60614   248-1761
Hours: Mon–Fri 10 am–8 pm, Sat & Sun 10 am–6 pm
CC: A, M, V

A sign on the window says "Fetching Garments" and when you enter this spacious shop that is exactly what you will see: racks and racks of very reasonably priced easy-to-wear fashions for women, some imported from India. Almost everything—socks, cotton underpants, scarves and belts—are made from natural fibers. The pantyhose are by Dim and Perry Ellis, and there are Esprit socks on occasion. The contemporary sportswear lines are by Esprit, Emmanuelle (a Dutch line), Reminiscence and Street Life. There are jackets, dresses, shirts, tops, skirts, pants and jeans. Sizes are junior 3 to 15, but there is a good selection for larger customers of loose tops and elastic-waisted skirts and pants: pregnant women frequently shop here. There is a nice display of inexpensive jewelry from India and from local suppliers in a range that goes up to $30. And there are large leather handbags in a price range from $18 to $40. So take a look at the fresh fashions carried by Phyllis McLennon and Betsey Nore in this shop which is, indeed, filled with Presence. –AT

PRESENCE ACTIVEWEAR

2467 N Clark / 60614   549-1716
Hours: Mon–Fri 10 am–8 pm, Sat 10 am–6 pm, Sun 11 am– 6 pm
CC: A, M, V

This complete source for exercise clothing was opened in 1983 by those enterprising women from Presence—Phyllis McLennon and Betsey Nore, who were banking on the continuing fitness craze. As at Presence the prices are moderate, and there is a good selection of glorified sweats by big-name manufacturers. The average price for a leotard is $20; for tights, $7. Everything for today's most fashionable workout is at Activewear, except shoes, which they do not stock. There are cotton turtlenecks ($11.75) and T-shirts and stirrup pants (about $20). –AT

RAYMOND HUDD

2545 N Clark / 60614   477-1159
2549 N Clark (evening, bridal wear)
Hours: Mon–Sat 11:30 am–6:30 pm, Closed Sun
CC: A, M, V

In the 35 years that Raymond Hudd has been designing women's hats, he has earned the title "The Mahatma of Mad Hatters." Both he and his classy hats survived the '60s and '70s when fashionable women stopped wearing hats along with corsets and little white gloves. Now in the '80s Raymond is busy placing 1500 hats a year on the heads of a new generation of hat-lovers. Raymond himself believes his continued popularity comes from his talent for "doing a mad, wild hat with sophistication and good taste."

Raymond's innovative designs have appealed to celebrities as diverse as Joan Crawford, Ann Landers and Phyllis Diller—who owns about 500 hats. Lee Phillip began her career as a TV weather woman. Raymond designed a hat a day for her for 365 days: each hat, without a single duplication, symbolized some aspect of the weather. One incorporated a boat, another a watermelon, a third a thermometer... Needless to say, both Lee and Raymond understandably profited from the publicity.

Raymond's hats are designed to attract attention; so if you want to be noticed buy a hat from the excellent selection that Raymond and his assistant, Tom Hopkins, have waiting for you. When we visited the shop at Easter, the hat stands were filled with a stunning array of flowery bonnets: pillboxes, cloches, fedoras and boaters, as well as hats with wide brims, derbies and the currently popular peek-a-boos. The shapes themselves are not unusual; it is the trimming that distinguishes a Raymond Hudd hat. He often chooses a theme, as he did recently to celebrate the 50th anniversary of the Brookfield Zoo. Little gray elephants marched across one hat, while cardinals seemed to be taking off from another. There were a dozen hats in the window, each with a pink flamingo perched on top.

Prices average from $60 to $100, and you get a lot for your money. Apart from his unique designs, Raymond's workmanship is impeccable. He buys the materials himself in New York and uses one trusted firm to make up the basic shapes. The winter materials are velour and wool felt. Raymond does not use synthetics because they do not absorb perspiration. He searches everywhere for trimmings, from flea markets to flower and toy shops. Then he and Tom create exciting, beautiful hats from the basic shapes.

Raymond grew up on a farm during the Depression—far away from the glamorous world of fashion. But he left in the '40s to see first-hand the big city he had heard about on the radio. Without any experience, he landed a job trimming hats at Goldblatt's. He opened his first store in the late '40s—a tiny space 100 feet square. He moved to elegant Oak Street in the '50s and thrived there until hats lost appeal in the '60s, when he closed the shop and ran a business wholesaling hats to Korshak's and Wieboldt's. Then in 1981 he opened his present shop.

Raymond says proudly that he has orders for 300 to 400 hats at all times. Not a single one of his hats has ever gone unsold: every one, from the black Halloween pillbox adorned with realistic spiders to the hat commemorating the first woman astronaut, is snatched up by women eager to be noticed at the opera, gallery-opening or a special party. He has opened a new shop next door, featuring hats for evening and bridal wear exclusively.

So stop by Raymond Hudd's to see what's new and

don't be surprised if you get started on a collection of zany, irresistible hats. –AT

RINGOLEVIO

2001 N Halsted / 60614   642-4999
Hours: Tues–Fri 11 am–9 pm, Sat 10 am–7 pm, Sun 12 am–6 pm, Closed Mon
CC: A, M, V

The design of this shop is as innovative as the clothes and accessories which are sold here. The owners describe the stock as "spirited unisex sportswear from around the world. " There are men's and women's unisex sweaters, pants and shirts. You can also buy the latest look in stationery, jewelry ($45 to $130) and various gift items. Ringolevio stays open late in spring and summer and offers merchandise with a new look in order to help make shopping what it was probably intended to be—fun! –AT

ROCKET 69

3180 N Clark / 60657   472-7878
Hours: Mon–Sat 11 am–7 pm, Sun 12 pm–5 pm
Halloween & Xmas 9 am–9 pm
CC: A, M, V, Disc

This store is a combination gift shop, art gallery, novelty store, clothing boutique, card shop and odds-and-ends emporium and it is really fun to visit. The owner, John Augustine, says he sells "Toys for the Young Professional." The toys are things like folding hair brushes, kaleidoscopes, rubber eyeballs which you can drop into somebody's drink, fake racks that glow in the dark and other weird things too numerous to mention. If your tastes don't run to the whimsical, you will be interested to know that John has 60 feet of greeting card racks, which include the largest selection of postcards in the city, and all kinds of greeting cards from sweet to sick and crazy. There are Betty Boop cards, balloons and Gary Larson cards. Sunglasses are available, and can be made to order. There is also hair dye in wild colors and makeup too. Then there are the clothes. There are, predictably, T-shirts and sweatshirts, but there are also vintage fashions for men and women in a price range from $9 to $50. Among the $50 items are jackets with lace collars.

There are new clothes too, all of them interesting. For instance, there is a sack dress made from parachute material: one size in this dress fits all, from small to extra-large. And there is jewelry. There is American Indian jewelry, and, says John, jewelry from Europe to Taiwan. Fifty dollars will buy you hand-beaded earrings. If you come to Rocket 69 with as little as $25 or as much as $75 you can go home with a purchase that is sure to give you many hours of pleasure. And take a good look at the store—especially the fire escape that John has attached as a kind of mural to the back wall! –AT

RUSSO

2209 N Halsted / 60614   348-8588
Hours: Mon–Fri 11 am–9 pm, Sat 11 am–8 pm, Sun 11 am–5 pm
CC: A, M, V

This is a new shoe store for men which carries also

clothing and accessories for men and women, located in a beautifully renovated brownstone right next door to Carlucci's Restaurant. Dresses by Irina Tarré are extraordinary: made of unusual fabrics, some mixed, and with a sophisticated European look, they come in bright colors and are often beaded and sequined. Prices start at $800. Accessories for women include handbags ($30 to $300) and jewelry both new and vintage European: Deco pins and necklaces run from $10 to $350. Russo does not carry women's shoes; but Italian shoes for men by Linea Aldo are soft leather, two-toned and slim-lined with a low-cut vamp. The Kenneth Cole shoe line is also carried here. Prices for these run $110 to $165. Russo carries better sportswear and evening wear and coats for men and women. –MC

SALAMANDER

2040 N Halsted / 60614   935-7447
Hours: Mon–Fri 11 am–7 pm, Sat 10 am–6 pm, Sun 12 pm–5 pm
CC: A, M, V

This store offers men's and women's sportswear that is conservative but contemporary, at moderate prices. In both winter and summer you will find an extensive collection of unique sweaters costing on the average about $50. The women's clothes use jewelry very well, and there are plenty of attractive necklaces and earrings on display here ($20 to $40). Men's clothes come from well-known companies in the moderate range like Henry Grethel and Robert Bruce for shirts, sweaters and some pants ($30 to $60). –AT

SATURDAY'S CHILD

2146 N Halsted / 60614   525-8697
50 E Washington / 60601   372-8697
Hours: Halsted: Mon–Wed 10 am–6 pm, Thurs & Fri
10 am–7 pm, Sat 10 am–6 pm, Sun 12 pm–5 pm.
Washington: Mon–Fri 10 am–6 pm, Sat 10 am–5 pm,
Closed Sun
CC: A, M, V

This is a toy store with a sense of tradition. There are educational and fine imported toys side-by-side with old favorites that generations of children have loved. Owner Marcia Nordine will special order for her devoted customers. Toys and books from major manufacturers and publishers are also found here. There is a play area for energetic tots with furniture and toys which can be ordered on request. Whatever you want for your child, you can find a quality version of it in this shop, in a charming setting. –AT

SILVER MOON

3337 N Halsted / 60657   883-0222
Hours: Sun–Tues 1 pm–5 pm, Wed–Sat 12 pm–6 pm
CC: A, M, V

This vintage shop glitters with pearls, rhinestones and sequins. Tari Costan, the owner, specializes in glamorous clothes for special occasions. There are cocktail dresses and ball gowns, turn-of-the-century wedding dresses made of silk rayon and silk chiffon, satin and cotton, are priced between $65 and $100. Silk beaded dresses are the most expensive.

The stock is large but selective. You can find '40s and '50s sweaters sewn with pearls and sequins ($35 to $50) which are very stylish now. Very pretty blouses with feminine ruffles and delicate little collars cost about $15.

There are clothes for men here too: tuxedos, tails and hard-to-find tuxedo shirts. The shirts, which go for about $20, come in a terrific variety of styles: some pleated, some ruffled, some plain, some with wing collars. There are men's trousers with pleats and wonderful smoking jackets—I saw one I loved in a deep plum corduroy with a plum velvet collar. But there are others in dark blue velvet, in deep burgundy silk, in brocade or in rayon. Some are figured and textured, some are plain. They all make you think of William Powell and Cary Grant on or off the set.

Everything in the shop is, of course, in perfect condition. If something is not up to her standard for any reason, Tari puts it in her small "as is" section where there are great bargains for anyone who likes to sew.

Some beautiful pieces are hung on the walls like paintings: an exquisite cut velvet shawl and a Victorian lace dress, for example. There is a lot of Art Nouveau and Art Deco jewelry, mostly metal and stones. Pieces range from $16 for earrings to $100 for a large bracelet.

If you have a formal occasion, try Silver Moon for a unique look. But try it anyway for fun. –MC

STEVE STARR STUDIOS

2654 N Clark / 60614   525-6530
Hours: Mon–Thurs 2 pm–6 pm, Fri 2 pm–5 pm,
Sat 12 pm–5 pm Winter Suns: 12 pm–5 pm, Summer Suns:
by chance
CC: M, V

Steve Starr has been selling Art Deco for almost half his life and you can see proof of that at his 18-year-old shop on Clark Street. 1986 is his 19th anniversary. The ceilings in the shop are high and the walls are covered with over 500 photographs both of customers like Diana Ross and Bette Midler and scenes from theatrical productions Steve has been connected with over the years. These photographs are in Art Deco frames from Steve's personal collection. The frames are not for sale, but other things are: a fine selection of restored furniture, glassware, lamps, costume jewelry at reasonable prices, and ashtrays culled from the U.S. and Europe, which attract collectors from around the world. The average price for a collectible is $40. And Steve does have striking reproductions of sconces, statues, wall reliefs, and vases which start at about $95. There is a beautiful shell console table hand-lacquered in shimmering colors which supports a plate-glass top priced at around $550. These reproductions really need to be seen to be appreciated. –AT

TOSHIRO

3309 N Clark / 60657   248-1487
Hours: Wed–Sat 12 pm–7 pm, Sun 12 pm–5 pm, Closed Mon & Tues
CC: A, M, V

Japanese designers are creating high fashion today with their loose-fitting, casual styles. At Toshiro, Nana and Roger Sullivan sell traditional Japanese clothing woven in indigo blues and earth colors at prices running from $35 to $400. More expensive items are made from carefully restored fabrics. The materials are hand-loomed cottons, and you will find kimonos (some decorated with hand-stitched quilting), padded jackets, over garments, shop coats, pants with elastic waists, and obis. The clothing is unisex. Toshiro does not carry any accessories but both Roger and Nana, who discovered the art of kasuri weaving when she was in Japan studying for a degree in Japanese history, plan to extend their stock to include contemporary Japanese clothing in the near future. Now the emphasis is on traditional garments, but the look that can be put together in this stunningly minimal shop is striking indeed. –MC

TRAFFICK

3313 N Broadway / 60657   549-1502
Hours: Mon–Fri 12 pm–7 pm, Sat 11 am–6 pm, Sun 12 pm–5 pm
CC: A, M, V

You can find casual clothes and clever gift items for men at reasonable prices here, and one really neat thing about this store is the aerobics and exercise department which sells everything a man could need, year 'round, for a workout. There are no running outfits, but there are tops, shorts, sweats and T-shirts, and women buy everything too. In fact Traffick considers that it has casual clothes for men *and* women, since everything is unisex, although basically designed for men. There is no outer wear, but there are socks, ties, scarves and gloves. Fabrics tend to be natural: wool and cotton. The stock differs completely in Fall and Spring. And don't forget Traffick for birthdays or Christmas. –AT

UNA RAMA DEL JARDIN

3407-9 N Clark / 60657   883-4443
Hours: Tues–Sat 12 pm–5 pm, Closed Sun & Mon
CC: A

This shop, which is like a typical market stall in the Zona Rosa in Mexico City, is jam-packed with Mexican imports. And the prices are almost as low as Mexican prices. I don't know how they do it! Straw shopping bags in dozens of bright colors cost only $9. Embroidered dresses of oaxaca silk and cotton start at $40. You can choose your Christmas tree ornaments from hundreds of straw and bread dough designs ($1 to $2.50). Don't forget to check out the wool and cotton shawls and the practical, comfortable and warm cotton jerga shirts ($10 to $20). Joe Ortiz, the owner, goes to Mexico in March, and in April the shop is open on Sundays as well from 12 to 4. –MC

UNDERTHINGS

804 W Webster / 60614   472-9291
Hours: Mon–Fri 12 pm–7 pm, Sat 11 am–6 pm, Closed Sun
CC: M, V

This pretty little shop specializes in practical but feminine lingerie—at undeniably high prices. Owner Molly Reynolds imports camisoles and panties from Italy, Switzerland and Germany. A lovely Hanro or Reposa camisole runs $15 and up. Lueme Italian panties vary in price, as do the shop's hard-to-find cotton half-slips. I loved one long, delicate one that cost $40. Cotton nightgowns go for around $50 and velour and terry cloth robes in bright colors will set you back $80. Poly-satin nightgowns, chemises and robes can go for as high as $200. You can buy long-wearing Dim panty hose from France in more than 20 shades for $3 and up. And there is a line of silk stretch briefs for men at $8. –MC

WHEEL AND DEAL

3515 N Halsted / 60657   871-7639
Hours: Wed, Thurs, Fri, Sat 1 pm–6 pm, Sun 1 pm–5
pm, Closed Mon & Tues
CC: M, V

This intriguing store specializes in folk art, Black Americana, Century of Progress memorabilia and railroad items from the past. Steve and Kalon Sloan's motto is, "We Like the Unusual." I saw a picture frame that was an example of "tramp art": it was made of orange crate slats intricately carved by a hobo or farm worker around the turn of the century, and it went for $60. Then there was a life-sized robot with a lighted head and a chest that opened to reveal a cabinet made by Steve himself. The railway items include lanterns, timetables, silverware and china, blankets and linens from Pullman cars. There are also ash trays and linens from old hotels. The window display recently was a magician's trick: sawing a woman in half. Everything in this shop is fun—whether it be pre-fifties furniture or old plastic jewelry. And prices are reasonable. –AT

WHISPERS LINGERIE

2441 N Clark / 60614   327-4422
Hours: Mon & Thurs 11 am–7 pm, Tues, Wed, Sat 11
am–6 pm, Closed Sun
CC: A, M, V

Jane Gregoris, the owner, makes it easy to buy from her enormous collection of romantic and/or daring lingerie. Service is personal and the shop, which used to be a barbershop, is charming, with its original tile shelving unit along one wall, its tin ceiling and antique fixtures. Jane considers this a lingerie gift shop, and she has more men than women customers, because she encourages men to enter her friendly shop, and she holds two men-only champagne fashion shows at Christmastime. In fact, Jane is adding men's robes to her normal stock of men's underwear.

There are three Whispers stores: this one in Chicago, one in Evanston and one in Northbrook. Family members manage all the stores, so you are assured of good service at all of them. Jane has always overstocked, so there are a huge number of sizes and styles from companies including Christian Dior and Olga. Every kind of bra can be found here, including running bras, and prices go from $9 to $25. I saw a delicate black lace bra and panty set with embroidered flowers and pearls for $16. More daring was a bra and matching garter belt in red silk for $40. There is a huge assortment of pantyhose, patterned, plain and in all colors. And Whispers has stockings as well as pantyhose: stockings and garter belts are often difficult to find. Camisoles, teddies and tap pants are very popular now; they come in silks, cottons and synthetics here, in pretty colors. Nightshirts are also "in": I loved an off-white silk one at $95: it looked like something Myrna Loy would use for elegant lounging. Among the more expensive items was a silk teddy for $65. But there are varying price ranges at Whispers so you can spend more or less what you have budgeted. Among the more unusual offerings are handbeaded cotton T-shirts and underwear at about $30 a set.

So come to Whispers for the latest in bold and demure lingerie and enjoy the pleasant, quaint atmosphere. –AT

CONSUELO'S

3931 N Ashland / 60613   935-7943
Hours: Tues–Sat 1 pm–6 pm
CC: Cash Or Check Only

This treasure-filled, uncluttered vintage shop has a wonderful theatrical look. It was planned that way by Consuelo Aguilar, the friendly, outgoing woman who started it in 1977. Consuelo, who grew up in the Pilsen section of Chicago, discovered the joys of vintage-hunting in the Bay Area in the late '60s when she was a student at San Francisco State. She owns the marvelous building at the corner of Ashland and Irving Park Road, with its high ceilings, ornate trims and beautiful old polished wood floors. The clothes are kept in antique cabinets, and when we were there Consuelo had lined up 18 wonderful '40s mannikin heads wearing vintage hats, all in a row across the tops of the dress cabinets. These great props were the first things that met our eyes and they were a knockout. No wonder artists and theatre people love to come to Consuelo's. In fact, the production people from Victory Gardens, Steppenwolf and Remains Theatre frequently get their costumes here.

The stock of dresses from the '40s and '50s is small but selective. Everything is in perfect condition, because Consuelo always makes sure of this before she buys at auctions and estate sales. These beautiful hand-made silk dresses and hand-painted rayon ones range in price from $18 to $20. That's the good news. The bad news is that most of them are no larger than size 10.

Those of us who are full-figured will fare better in the blouse section, where we can find garments that could have been worn 30 years ago by Jayne Mansfield or Marilyn Monroe. But you had better be ready to unearth your full slips or camisoles because the best blouses are nylon sheers. But there are also lovely delicate summer blouses from the '60s.

Unisex Hawaiian shirts run from $5 to $15, depending on the original quality of the material. And we bought chic '40s light wool flannel jackets, with little Mexican people and little cactuses embroidered on them, for $20 apiece. A real bargain! And remember that Lily Ann coat you discarded in 1965 when you switched to denim? Well, you can buy it back from Consuelo for $25, if you really miss it now.

The jewelry—plastics, bakelite, some rhinestones—is modestly priced.

For fashion-conscious men Consuelo has overcoats, never worn, from the '40s, and suits from the '20s through the '50s. John Malkevitch has been known to shop here. And why not? The ambiance is charming, and Consuelo herself is very pleasant, and comfortable to be around. She will let you browse to your heart's content, or if you feel like chatting, she will pull out chairs from the back of the shop—where she has an apartment—and perhaps offer you tea in depression glassware. So go to the Lakeview area—which is experiencing an urban renaissance—and pay a visit to Consuelo. -MC

RENAISSANCE BUTTONS*

7009 N Sheridan Rd / 60626   465-0711
Hours: Tues–Sat 1 pm–6 pm, Closed Sun & Mon
CC: Cash Or Check Only

Sarah Trezevant sells old and new buttons in this small shop, both wholesale and retail, all over the country. She buys most of her buttons in Europe, but some come from warehouse sales in the U.S. Her customers are button collectors, tailors, and buyers and sellers of vintage clothing. Large round celluloid buttons, perfect to liven up an old jacket or coat, are a bargain at $1.50.

Enamelled buttons, both old and new, are popular. New ones are around $1.75 each and old ones run from $2 to $25 apiece for special ones. Half Sarah's customers make jewelry from their buttons. In addition to buttons, Sarah also sells white lace collars and exquisite pieces of antique lace. –MC
*(*Note at press time—moved to Evanston 475-5262)*

STUDIO SEW SEW

5412 N Clark / 60640   989-4200
Hours: Mon–Sat 1:30 pm–6:30 pm Closed Sun,
Note: call before you come
CC: Cash Or Check Only

This shop, owned by Leah Missbach and Dawn Hurwitz, is in an office loft on the second floor of a former theatre building. Dawn, a fashion designer who sells to shops like Artwear, provides original designs for Studio Sew Sew. Leah is also a designer, but her speciality, as an expert tailor, is making over vintage clothes.

Leah has racksful of men's suits from the '40s and '50s that run about $50. Men can buy them off the rack and Leah will alter them for a few dollars. But if a woman wants a man's suit because she admires the fabric and the look, Leah will redo it completely so that it looks and fits like a woman's suit. The charge for this complete remodeling is $50. You can bring in a suit you bought elsewhere and Leah will redo it for the same price.

Dawn makes comfortable pants, dresses, shirts, skirts and jumpsuits from cotton, corduroy and wool. Some are one-size-fits-all. She will make these to order for you in your own style, color and size, from $40, in a couple of weeks. You can take a fabric swatch with you in case you want to match up accessories. You can pick up some funky ones here too, made by local artists. Campy tie-dyed anklets are $7; brass earrings decorated with leather and beads go for $18.

When they're not working in the shop and its workroom Leah and Dawn are out combing vintage shops and visiting estate sales. They have a large selection of men's and women's evening wear. You can rent one of these garments for $20, or Leah can turn an old ball gown into a contemporary masterpiece for about $40—$20 if it is only a jacket.

So—you can have your own couturiére at bargain basement prices at Studio Sew Sew! –MC

WILD GOOSE CHASE QUILT GALLERY

6977 N Sheridan Rd / 60626   465-8787
Hours: Daily: 12 pm–6 pm, Closed Sun
CC: Cash Only

This shop moved recently from Evanston to this far north location. A few of the quilts are over 100 years old, but most of them were made about 25 to 50 years ago. There are appliqués, comforters and cozy quilts with prices starting at $50. The hundreds of patterns include the double wedding ring, delectable mountain and grandmother's flower garden. Owner Marilyn Packer also sells hooked and braided rugs and pretty dolls made from antique fabrics. -MC

INDIA SARI PALACE

2534 W Devon / 60659   338-2127
Hours: 11 am–8 pm Daily, Closed Tues
CC: M, V

This is a branch of a national company which provides materials for clothing for East Indian women living in the United States. The traditional dress are the sari and the salwar-kameez, a two-piece garment that is a shirt and long trousers. The selection of fabrics here is enormous: there are raw Indian silks, pure French silks and chiffons and Japanese polyesters. You can buy ready-made clothes here too: dupddas, which are chiffon scarves for the shoulders, and garments which run small, medium and large at a price range of $15 to $45. The fabrics run $1.99 to $4.99 a yard. A salwar-kameez could be made up for between $45 and $150, and silk saris at a range of $75 to $400. Generally a sari takes six yards of material. The helpful staff here gives lessons in sari dressing and provides an instruction sheet you can take home. There are other sari shops on Devon Avenue, but the Sari Palace seems to offer the largest selection of materials.
–MC

ROSEMARY'S CHUBBY GIRLS SHOP

2607 W Devon / 60659   743-8831
Hours: Mon & Thurs 12 pm–8 pm, Tues, Wed, Fri, Sat 10 am–5 pm, Closed Sun
CC: M, V

This shop is one of the few places in the city where you can find attractive clothes in girls' half sizes. Designer label children's lines are now available in half-sizes and Joyce Buehling, Rosemary's owner, carries many of them. Clothes in sizes $8^{1}/_{2}$ to $16^{1}/_{2}$ have waist lines that run from $20^{1}/_{2}$ to $28^{1}/_{2}$. Joyce carries Wrangler jeans, bathing suits, slips, bras and panties—all priced, as you would expect, slightly higher than garments in regular sizes. When I asked her about the shop's name, Joyce said she realized that young girls do not like to be called chubby, but she wants to tell it like it is, and to demonstrate that chubby girls' clothes do not have to be utilitarian. Rosemary's has a mail order brochure which makes shopping here more convenient. Call Joyce if you want one. –MC

THE SWEDEN SHOP

3304 W Foster / 60625
Hours: Tues, Wed, Fri, Sat 9:30 am–6 pm, Mon &
Thurs 9:30 am–9 pm, Closed Sun
CC: M, V

Amid the beautiful imported items in this shop, you will find an unusual collection of clogs. Ingrid Bergstrom, the owner, says she has 2000 pairs stashed away in her back room, so that you can find the size, color and style you are looking for. Adult clogs run between $25 and $35, while children's sizes go for $15 to $20. The handcrafted jewelry here is designed by the Norwegian artist David Anderson; here are pendants and rings in silver, some with stones, some with enamel, priced from $25 to $150. In the winter Ingrid has a complete selection of handmade Norwegian wool sweaters for men, women and children. There are interesting kitchen items here, as well as delicately painted Porsgrund dishes from Norway, and a large selection of Scandinavian gift items, like popular handpainted figurines which sell for $10 to $30, *dalanasten* or dala horses, blue and red painted wooden horses in varying sizes, which are a traditional Swedish good luck gift, tree ornaments of straw and wood ($2 to $5) and crystal tree ornaments ($10 to $25). You'll also find an attractive array of Swedish (naturally) china and glassware with famous names at reasonable prices. Don't forget that The Sweden Shop also has a gift catalogue. And while you're here, try lunch at the Swedish Cafe and Pastry Market across the street, where you can also buy delicious eatables like limpa bread. –MC

ARTISANS 21

5225 S Harper Court / 60615   288-7450
Hours: Tues–Fri 12 pm–5 pm, Sat 10 am–5 pm, Sun 12 pm–4 pm
CC: Cash Or Check Only

This shop is run by the artisans and artists who make the merchandise. You can find pottery here and papier maché and fabric art, photographs, woven goods, dolls, clothing and much more. Handwoven jackets, shawls, dresses, sweaters and tie-dyed and painted shirts for adults are expensive but beautifully made. There are quilted sashes ($15–$20) and dresses ($50–$100). There is interesting jewelry in silver, brass, and some ceramic and some painted jewelry, and there are a variety of painted and photographic greeting cards. The walls are covered with paintings and framed photographs done by the owners, the majority of whom live in Hyde Park and South Shore. This is a great place to buy unusual gifts. -MC

INGRID'S WEARABLE ART

5211 S Harper Court / 60615   955-2727
Hours: Tues–Sat 11 am–5:30 pm, Closed Sun, Mon
CC: A

Ingrid Grimes is a former designer of theatrical costumes who has brought her art to the general public. She will design and produce virtually any garment you want and will work closely with you during the production period to make sure you are satisfied. If you like, her illustrator will draw the garment on paper for you so that everyone is clear about exactly what you want. Ingrid has a variety of beautiful Italian fabrics in stock, but you can bring in your own material if you wish. (You can also choose from Ingrid's large selection of patterns.) An evening dress will cost about $300 with Ingrid's material and about half that if you provide your own.

I like the glamorous chemises and camisoles that Ingrid carries as regular merchandise. She will custom design these for you too if you prefer. A black silk bias-cut camisole with hand beading, made to order for you, costs $65. For the same amount you can get a hand-painted sweatshirt. I ordered one with a colorful tiger design and sequins. It takes a few weeks to get the sweatshirts and about ten days for the camisoles and chemises.

Ingrid likes the glamorous look of the '20s and '30s, and she also specializes in exciting clothes for the larger woman—an important service.

In one of the shop's interesting antique cabinets you will find hand-painted leather goods from Marvin Sin, a Washington D.C. designer. The bags have a beautiful black woman's face painted against a dark background. Sin's key chains run about $20, but a briefcase can go as high as $600. If you want to spend the money, you can be sure you won't see yourself coming and going. Marvin Sin will make bags to order, but Ingrid must first have an illustration drawn and sent to him, so it takes a little time.

Another line exclusive with Ingrid are the jewelry and belts made by Babatunde, a Chicago artist. Her large brass earrings run $25 to $100 and her beautiful hand-worked belts go up to $250.

There are some pretty Italian scarves, which Ingrid brought back from Italy, at $30.

This shop is frankly expensive and only for women who are willing to pay for a unique look. -MC

MAXINES

1507 E 53rd St / 60615   241-6447
1613 E 87th St / 60617   221-8308
Hours: 53rd St: Mon–Sat 10 am–6 pm, Closed Sun
87th St: Mon–Sat 10 am–7 pm, Sun 12 pm–
5 pm
CC: M, V, Disc

These two shops run by Maxine Livingston and her daughter Brenda, provide clothing in a large range of sizes: suits, dresses, sportswear and evening wear from size 3 to size 24½. Popular sequined blouses are $100 and Harvé Benard suits and coats run $100 to $300. There are plenty of accessories, including shoes, at medium prices, handbags and hats. This is a real head-to-toe operation, but the emphasis here is on half-size clothes for the large woman. -MC

TOYS ET CETERA

5206 S Harper / 60615   324-6039
Hours: Mon–Sat 9:30 am–5:30 pm, Sunday 12 pm–
5 pm
CC: M, V

Owner Nancy Stanek stocks every kind of game or toy imaginable, in addition to the usual panoply of commercial toys like Playskool and Brio. She has professional artists supplies from Carandache in Switzerland and unique Ravensburger German puzzles. The largest puzzle, which is guaranteed to drive you out of your mind, has 12,000 pieces and sells for $100. Unusual dolls, which are really for collectors, can be given to little children. There are realistic Gotz German dolls and French babyfaced ones. You can buy little toys here for less than $1 and elaborate toys, games and dolls for as much as $400. –MC

ALLISON'S LA PARISIENNE

8834 S Cottage Grove / 60619   994-8975
Hours: Mon–Sat 10 am–6:30 pm, Closed Sun
CC: A, D, V

Myrtle Allison's elegantly furnished little shop carries expensive, carefully selected women's clothing. There are Hannae Mori red print sweaters for $500, leather and suede dresses in solid bright colors with full, straight or trumpet skirts which start at $400, hand-painted silk dresses running between $350 and $1500. Suits and two-piece dresses in silk lace brocade, perfect for formal occasions, will set you back about $1000. Barbara Kates is one of Allison's designers. There is an interesting jewelry collection displayed in attractive antique cases.

Allison's La Parisienne caters to a discriminating clientele which includes Joan Johnson, the wife of the president of Johnson Products, Helen Maybelle, the owner of the Soul Queen Restaurant and Essie Kupcinet. Sizes in the shop run only as high as 16, which in designer clothes is usually larger than in less expensive models. –MC

THE KENSINGTON SHOPPE

7101 S Yates Blvd / 60649   221-9727
Hours: Winter months, Mon–Sat 10 am–6 pm, Closed Sun, June, July, Aug, Sept, Mon–Sat 12 pm–6 pm, Sun 12 pm–5 pm
CC: A, V, M

It's worth a drive to South Shore, if you don't already live near there, to see the extensive collection of beautiful objects from all over the world, but particularly from Africa, in this spacious, airy shop. We saw a four-foot-tall Nimba statue made by the Baga people of Guinea in West Africa. It was stunning, and it sold for $6000. There are many less expensive pieces: a wide variety of masks, for instance. I admired one, a helmet mask from Zaire, made of tiger and goat hair on wood. There are masks from Mali, Nigeria and the Ivory Coast. You can buy a one-of-a kind artifact for as little as $5 or $15.

And there is handmade jewelry from Africa and from South America. We saw large African ebony earrings, and other earrings made from combinations of cherry, walnut and Brazilian purple heart. There were malachite necklaces from Mali, and many ivory pieces from the southeast and southwest coasts of Africa. And more! Next to the jewelry lay beautiful bags and belts from Senegal, fashioned from python, crocodile and iguana, which certainly invited favorable comparison with Italian leatherwork.

Everywhere we looked, we saw beautiful pieces: a Peruvian rug, a colorful Kente cloth (they make pretty belts), a South American wall hanging...Helen Hull, the manager of the shop, told us that the price range is from fifty cents to —of course—$6000.

The Kensington Shoppe was opened in 1982 by the owners, Moses and Rosalind Harris. Rosalind had had an interior design studio on the second floor since 1979. Moses had been Director of Human Resources at G.D. Searle Co. before he went to school to learn more about interior design, which was his first love. When he got his degree he bought the building on Yates Blvd., and then traveled extensively, looking for artifacts. He became knowledgeable about Africa in particular, and acquired sources in those countries which supply him with the beautiful African art objects in the intriguing Henderson Gallerie. The shop also has an exotic plant section, a section where kitchen and dining accessories are on sale...in fact, you can buy everything from American-made ceramics to stone carvings of everyday life in Nigeria from Moses and Rosalind.

So hop down to Yates Boulevard—a fifteen or twenty minute drive from the Loop—and enjoy yourself. –AT

MAXINES

1613 E 87th St / 60617   221-8308
(See listing under South)

THOMAS MOORE

1623 E 87th St / 60617   768-5600
1708 E 87th St / 60617   721-7900 (Formal Wear)
Hours: 1623: Mon–Sat 10 am–7 pm, Sun 11 am–5 pm
1708: Mon–Sat 10 am–7 pm, Closed Sun
CC: A, C, D, M, V

Partners Cylus Thomas and Eric Moore have been in the men's clothing business for more than a decade and they have an enormous inventory of designer apparel. They have hard-to-find Borsalino and Dobbs hats ($90–$150), Missoni and Fumagalli silk ties ($25–$60) and the largest selection of reptile-skin shoes in bright and neutral colors in the city ($200–$600). There are even ostrich skin shoes ($650), and soft leather jackets by Marc Buchanan and Gerry Wong ($250 & up).

Their large suit selection covers a wide price range. Suits by Givenchy, Valentino, Corneliani, Lanirossi, Marzotto and Brioni run from $300 to $2000 and there are plenty of high quality Italian sports shirts, slacks and sweaters by De Pietri, La Squadra and Cezar. Large and tall sizes are a specialty, so many well-known athletes shop here—Quentin Daly, Reggie Theus, Denis McKinnon—as does Mayor Harold Washington.

Across the street is Thomas Moore's well-stocked formal wear shop, where you can buy tuxedos by the likes of Bill Blass, Dynasty and YSL. Tuxedos come not only in black, white and beige, but also fuschia, bright yellow and orange. Prices start at $250. If you want to rent a tux for a weekend, it will cost between $50 and $75, and you can choose from more than 20 different formal looks, complete with matching cummerbund, bow tie and silk pocket square. If you are planning a wedding you can avail yourself of Thomas Moore's free color-coordinating service, which provides consultations with everyone in the wedding party to prevent clashing colors, unless you specifically want them. –MC

MERCHANDISE GUIDE

CODE: (M) Men
(W) Women
(C) Children
(V) Vintage
(A) Activewear

See pages 137-139 for page numbers

ACCESSORIES
(Belts, scarves, ties, etc)

Accents Studio (W)
Anastasia (W)
Art Effect (W)
Artisans 21 (M & W)
Banana Republic
  (M & W)
Blake (W)
Boutique Caprice (W)
Burdi (M & W)
City (W)
Clark Street Waltz (W)
Dégagé
Dei Giovani (M)
Divine Idea (M & W)
Elle Boutique (W)
Handle With Care (W)
Indulgence (W)
Intrinsic (M & W)
Jâcher (W)
Latham Ltd (W)

Mary Walter (W)
My Own Two Feet (C)
My Sister's Circus/Isis
  (W)
Nonpareil (W)
Panache Handbags
  & Accessories (W)
Port of Entry (W)
Presence (W)
Rowbottoms
  & Willoughby
  (M & W)
Russo (M & W)
Salamander (M & W)
Traffick (M & W)
Ultimo (M & W)

AFRICAN ARTIFACTS

The Baobab Tree
The Kensington
  Shoppe
Les Primitifs
Primitive Arts Ltd

ART DECO FURNITURE, GIFTS, ART OBJECTS

Flashy Trash
Fly-By-Nite Gallery
A Joint Venture
State Street Collection
Steve Starr Studios
Studio V

ART DECO REPRODUCTIONS, FURNITURE, ART OBJECTS

Etcetera
Steve Starr Studios
Studio V

ART OBJECTS: Art Nouveau

Fly-By-Nite Gallery

ART OBJECTS: Ethnic, Primitive

A Joint Venture
Les Primitifs
The Yeshe Collection

ART OBJECTS: Contemporary

Artisans 21

Beggars Market Ltd
A Joint Venture
Nonpareil
Pavo Real
The Yeshe Collection

ART OBJECTS: Vintage

Boomerang
Fly-By-Nite Gallery
Gloria
A Joint Venture
Steve Starr Studios
Studio V
Wheel and Deal

BALLET SHOES

A Capriccio
Enchanté

BALLOONS

Balloons To You
Rocket 69

BAR ACCESSORIES

Chiasso

BATH ACCESSORIES

City

BLACK AMERICANA

Wheel & Deal

BLANKETS

Erinisle
Pavo Real
Wheel & Deal (V)

BUTTONS

Renaissance Buttons

CHILDREN'S BOOKS

Goodies
Nonpareil
Saturday's Child

CHILDREN'S FURNITURE

Saturday's Child

CHILDREN'S SHOES

Beggars Market Ltd
   (Infants)
My Own Two Feet
Over the Rainbow

CHILDREN'S WEAR

All Our Children

Beggars Market Ltd
Handle With Care
Modalisque
My Own Two Feet
Over the Rainbow
Rosemary's Chubby
   Girls Shop
Sugar Magnolia

CHINA & EARTHENWARE

Boomerang (V)
Crate & Barrel
Jean Charles
   la Mode a Deux
Mexican Folk Art
The Sweden Shop
Studio V

COATS: *See MEN'S COATS and WOMEN'S COATS*

COSTUMES

Chicago Costume Co.

CRUISEWEAR

A Capriccio (W)
Apropos (A)
Giuseppe (M)
Latham Ltd (W)

CRUISEWEAR
Continued

My Sister's Circus/Isis
  (W)

CRYSTAL: *See GLASSWARE*

DANCEWEAR

A Capriccio
Presence Activewear

DRESSMAKERS CUSTOM DESIGN

Ingrid's Wearable Art
Staara
Studio Sew Sew

FLATWARE

Boomerang (V)
Crate & Barrel
The Sweden Shop

FOLK ARTS

Wheel & Deal

FURNITURE: New

City
Crate & Barrel
Nonpareil

FURNITURE: Vintage

Boomerang
Etcetera
Steve Starr Studios
Studio V
Wheel & Deal

GAMES

Chiasso
Toys Et Cetera

GIFTS

Accent Chicago
Artisans 21
Beggars Market Ltd
Chiasso
Crate & Barrel
Erinisle
Etcetera
A Joint Venture
Mexican Folk Arts
Nonpareil
Omiyage Ltd
Primitive Arts Ltd
Ringolevio
Una Rama del Jardin
The Sweden Shop

GLASSWARE

Accent Chicago

Clark Street Waltz
Crate & Barrel
Erinisle
Jean Charles
   la Mode a Deux
Mexican Folk Arts
State Street Collection
Steve Starr Studios
The Sweden Shop

GLOVES: New

Clark Street Waltz (W)
The Divine Idea (W)
Indulgence (W)
Rowbottoms
   & Willoughby
   (M & W)
Traffick (M)
Ultimo (M & W)

GLOVES: Vintage

The Divine Idea
Flashy Trash

GREETING CARDS

Artisans 21
Balloons To You
Beggars Market Ltd

Chiasso
A Joint Venture
Paper & Co.
Rocket 69
Studio V
The Sweden Shop

HANDBAGS

Accents Studio
Banana Republic
Battaglia
Boutique Caprice
City
Crate & Barrel
Gloria (V)
Indulgence
Ingrid's Wearable Art
The Kensington
   Shoppe
Lori's (discount)
Maxine's
Mexican Folk Arts
   (woven, fiber)
Panache Handbags
   & Accessories
Pavo Real
   (woven, fiber)
Presence
Russo
S'Agaro
Ultimo

HATS: New

Beggars Market Ltd
  (W)
Blake (W)
Burdi (W)
Clark Street Waltz (W)
Elle Boutique (W)
Erinisle (M & W)
Handle With Care (W)
Indulgence (W)
Maxine's (W)
Nonpareil (W)
Raymond Hudd (W)
Thomas Moore (M)
Ultimo (M & W)

HATS: Vintage

The Divine Idea
  (M & W)
Gloria (M & W)
Modalisque (W)
Studio V (W)

IRISH IMPORTS

Erinisle

INDIAN (EAST) CLOTHES

India Sari Palace

JAPANESE ARTIFACTS

The Yeshe Collection

JAPANESE CLOTHING

Omiyage Ltd
Over the Rainbow (C)
Toshiro
Ultimo
The Yeshe Collection

JEWELRY: Antique

Flashy Trash
Fly-By-Nite Gallery
Silver Moon

JEWELRY: Art Deco, Victorian Reproductions

Apropos
Port of Entry
Primitive Arts Ltd
Russo

JEWELRY: Costume

Anastasia
Apropos
Beggars Market Ltd
Blake
The End of the Line

Etcetera
Goodies
Indulgence
Jâcher
Mary Walter
Mexican Folk Arts
One Plus One
Panache Handbags
  & Accessories
Presence
Ringolevio
Rowbottoms
  & Willoughby
Russo
Salamander
Sugar Magnolia
Ultimo

JEWELRY: Ethnic

Boomerang
The Kensington
  Shoppe
Nonpareil
Presence
Les Primitifs
Primitive Arts Ltd
Rocket 69

JEWELRY: Designer, Handmade

Accents Studio

Allison's La Parisienne
Art Effect
Artisans 21
Chiasso
Clark Street Waltz
Dégagé
Elle Boutique
Handle With Care
Indulgence
Ingrid's Wearable Art
Intrinsic
The Kensington
  Shoppe
Mary Walter
Modalisque
My Sister's Circus/Isis
Omiyage Ltd
Port of Entry
Sugar Magnolia
The Sweden Shop
The Yeshe Collection

JEWELRY REPAIR

Accents Studio

JEWELRY: Vintage

Beggars Market Ltd
Boomerang
Clark Street Waltz
Consuelo's
Divine Idea

JEWELRY: Vintage Continued

Flashy Trash
Fly-By-Nite Gallery
Gloria
Goodies
A Joint Venture
Modalisque
Omiyage Ltd
Russo
Silver Moon
Steve Starr Studios
State Street Collection
Studio V
Wheel & Deal

KIMONOS

Clark Street Waltz
The Divine Idea
Toshiro
The Yeshe Collection

KITCHENWARE

Crate & Barrel
Goodies (V)
Omiyage Ltd (V)
State Street Collection (V)
Studio V (V)
The Sweden Shop

LAMPS

Boomerang (V)
Chiasso
City
Crate & Barrel
Etcetera
Steve Starr Studios (V)
Studio V (V)

LARGE WOMEN

Anastasia
Handle With Care
Ingrid's Wearable Art
Jâcher
Maxine's
My Sister's Circus/Isis
One Plus One
Panache Handbags
   & Accessories
Port of Entry
Presence
Rosemary's Chubby
   Girls Shop (C)
Staara
   (lingerie, pantyhose)
Studio Sew Sew

LATIN AMERICAN ARTIFACTS

Mexican Folk Arts

Pavo Real
Primitive Arts Ltd

LINENS

City
Crate & Barrel
Wheel & Deal

LINGERIE

Apropos
Art Effect
La Coquette
Enchanté
Flashy Trash (V)
Gloria (V)
Handle With Care
Ingrid's Wearable Art
Staara
Underthings
Whispers

MAKEUP, HAIR DYE

Accents Studio
Chicago Costume Co.
Rocket 69
Staara

MASKS

Chicago Costume Co.
Etcetera

Indulgence
The Kensington
   Shoppe
Les Primitifs
The Yeshe Collection

MATERNITY CLOTHES

Re Creations
   Maternity Shop
Presence
   (adaptable clothes)

MEN'S COATS

Consuelo's (V)
Dei Giovani
Gloria (V)
I.K. Don
Jean Charles
   la Mode a Deux
Rowbottoms &
   Willoughby
Russo

MEN'S CLOTHING:
New

Banana Republic
Burdi
Dei Giovani
Giuseppe
I.K. Don

MEN'S CLOTHING: New—Continued

In Rare Form
Intrinsic
Jean Charles
    la Mode a Deux
Ringolevio
Rowbottoms
    & Willoughby
Salamander
Thomas Moore's
    Men's Clothing
Toshiro
Traffick
Ultimo

MEN'S CLOTHING: Vintage

Consuelo's
The Divine Idea
Flashy Trash (V)
Gloria
Modalisque
Rocket 69
Silver Moon
Studio Sew Sew
Studio V

MEN'S SHOES

Banana Republic

Flashy Trash
Jean Charles
    la Mode a Deux
Russo
Thomas Moore

MEXICAN ARTIFACTS

Mexican Folk Arts
Pavo Real
Una Rama del Jardin

OFFICE ACCESSORIES

Crate & Barrel
Chiasso
City

ORIENTAL ARTIFACTS

A Joint Venture
The Yeshe Collection

PARTY GOODS

Balloons To You
Paper & Co.

POSTCARDS

Rocket 69

POSTERS

Accent Chicago

Fly-By-Nite Gallery
Studio V

POTTERY, CERAMICS

Artisans 21
Beggars Market Ltd
Boomerang
Crate & Barrel
Erinisle
Flashy Trash
Gloria
The Kensington
   Shoppe
Mexican Folk Arts
Omiyage Ltd
Les Primitifs
The Sweden Shop

QUILTS

Crate & Barrel
Wild Goose Chase
   Quilt Gallery

RAILROAD
MEMORABILIA
Wheel & Deal

RAINCOATS

Banana Republic
   (M & W)

Dei Giovani (M)
Rowbottoms
   & Willoughby

RENTAL CLOTHES

Chicago Costume Co.
   (M & W)
Studio Sew Sew
   (M & W)
Thomas Moore
   Formal Clothes (M)

RESORT WEAR—
See CRUISEWEAR

RUGS

Boomerang (V)
The Kensington
   Shoppe
Nonpareil
Pavo Real
Les Primitifs
Primitive Arts Ltd
Wild Goose Chase
   Quilt Gallery

SHAWLS

Artisans 21
Beggars Market Ltd
Clark Street Waltz

SHAWLS Continued

Erinisle
India Sari Palace
Pavo Real
Una Rama del Jardin
Ultimo

SLEEPWEAR: Women

All Our Children (C)
Apropos
   (W & C winter only)
La Coquette
Handle With Care
Underthings
Whispers

SOAPS, LOTIONS

City
Handle With Care

SOCKS, PANTYHOSE

Apropos
Art Effect
Beggars Market Ltd
Boutique Caprice
La Coquette
Latham Ltd
Lori's
My Own Two Feet
S'Agaro

Staara
This Little Piggy
Whispers

STATIONERY

Beggars Market Ltd
Chiasso
Paper & Co.
Ringolevio
The Sweden Shop

STOCKINGS—
(Not pantyhose)

Boutique Caprice
La Coquette
Enchanté
This Little Piggy
Whispers

SWEATERS:
Handmade

Art Effect
Artisans 21
Beggars Market Ltd
Dégagé
Dei Giovani
Gloria
Handle With Care
In Rare Form
Intrinsic
Jâcher

Pavo Real
Rowbottoms
  & Willoughby
The Sweden Shop
Ultimo

TABLEWEAR

Crate & Barrel
Boomerang (V)
Beggars Market Ltd
Studio V
The Sweden Shop
Wheel & Deal

TELEPHONES: Vintage

State Street Collection
Studio V

TEXTILES

Crate & Barrel
Indian Sari Palace
Les Primitifs
The Yeshe Collection

TOYS

Apropos
Artisans 21
Beauty and the Beast
Goodies (some V)
A Joint Venture

My Own Two Feet
Nonpareil
Saturday's Child
Wild Goose Chase
  Quilt Gallery
The Yeshe Collection

UNISEX CLOTHING

Artisans 21
Banana Republic
Blake
Consuelo's
Divine Idea
Giuseppe
In Rare Form
Intrinsic
Jean Charles
  la Mode a Deux
Mexican Folk Arts
Pavo Real
Ringolevio
Sugar Magnolia
Toshiro
Traffick

WALL HANGINGS

The Kensington
  Shoppe
Mexican Folk Arts
Pavo Real
Les Primitifs
Primitive Arts Ltd

WATCHES

Chiasso
Flashy Trash
Etcetera
Gloria
Nonpareil

WIGS

Chicago Costume Co.
Indulgence

WOMEN'S COATS

Anastasia
Benetton's
Consuelo's (V)
Dei Giovani
Elle Boutique
Erinsisle
Gloria (V)
Jean Charles
    la Mode a Deux
Maxine's
Russo

WOMEN'S
NEW CLOTHES:
Casual

Apropos
Artisans 21
Banana Republic

Benetton's
Blake
End of the Line
Handle With Care
Jâcher
Jean Charles
    la Mode a Deux
Mary Walter
Maxine's
Mexican Folk Arts
My Sister's Circus/Isis
Nonpareil
One Plus One
Panache Handbags
    & Accessories
Pavo Real
Port of Entry
Presence
Sugar Magnolia

WOMEN'S
NEW CLOTHES:
Career

Boutique Caprice
Dégagé
Latham Ltd
Mary Walter
Maxine's
Port of Entry

WOMEN'S
NEW CLOTHES:
Elegant

Allison's La Parisienne
Battaglia
Boutique Caprice
Burdi
Mary Walter
Staara
Ultimo

WOMEN'S
NEW CLOTHES:
Evening

Allison's La Parisienne
Boutique Caprice
Indulgence
Maxine's
Ultimo

WOMEN'S
NEW CLOTHES:
Fashion Forward

Anastasia
Art Effect
Blake
City
Handle with Care
Indulgence
My Sister's Circus/Isis
Ultimo

WOMEN'S
NEW CLOTHES:
Sportswear/
Activewear

Apropos
A Capriccio (A)
Banana Republic
Dégagé
End of the Line
Giuseppe (A)
Latham Ltd
Presence
Presence Activewear
   (A)
Ringolevio
Rosemary's Chubby
   Girls Shop (C)
Rowbottoms
   & Willoughby
Salamander
Sugar Magnolia

WOMEN'S NEW SHOES

Banana Republic
Battaglia
Boutique Caprice
Jean Charles
   la Mode a Deux
Lori's (discount)
Maxine's
S'Agaro

WOMEN'S VINTAGE CLOTHES

Clark Street Waltz
Consuelo's
Divine Idea
Flashy Trash
Gloria
Modalisque
Rocket 69
Silver Moon
State Street Collection

WOMEN'S VINTAGE SHOES

Gloria

ALPHABETICAL INDEX TO SHOPS

A

A Capriccio 15
Accent Chicago 15
Accents Studio 16
Allison's
    La Parisienne 117
All Our Children 61
Anastasia 61
Apropos 62
Art Effect 17
Artisans 21 113

B

The Baobob Tree 63
Ballons To You 63
Banana Republic 18
Battaglia 19
Beauty and the Beast 21
Beggars Market Ltd. 22
Benetton's 23
Blake 64
Boomerang 65
Boutique Caprice 24
Burdi 25

C

Chiasso 26
Chicago Costume
    Company 66
City 27
Clark Street Waltz 67
Consuelo's 103
La Coquette 80
Crate & Barrel 28

D

Dégagé 68
Dei Giovani 68
Divine Idea 69

E

Elle Boutique 70
Enchanté 31
End of the Line 31
Erinisle 72
Etcetera 32

F

Flashy Trash 73
Fly-By-Nite Gallery 33

G

Giuseppe 74
Gloria 75
Goodies 77

H

| Handle With Care | 34 |

I

I.K. Don	77
In Rare Form	35
India Sari Palace	109
Indulgence	78
Ingrid's Wearable Art	113
Intrinsic	36

J

Jâcher	79
Jean Charles La Mode A Deux	38
A Joint Venture	39

K

| The Kensington Shoppe | 117 |

L

Latham Ltd	39
This Little Piggy	55
Lori's Designer Shoes	39

M

Mary Walter	40
Maxine's	115
Mexican Folk Arts	82
Modalisque	11
My Own Two Feet	83
My Sister's Circus/ Isis	42

N

| Nonpareil | 84 |

O

Omiyage Ltd	83
One Plus One	43
Over The Rainbow	44

P

Panache Handbags & Accessories	86
Paper & Company	45
Pavo Real	45
Port of Entry	86
Presence	88
Presence Activewear	89
Les Primitifs	81
Primitive Arts Ltd	46

R

Una Rama Del Jardin	99
Raymond Hudd	89
Recreations Maternity Shop	47
Renaissance Buttons	104
Ringolevio	92
Rocket 69	92
Rosemary's Chubby Girls Shop	109
Rowbottoms & Willoughby	47
Russo	93

S

S'Agaro	49
Salamander	94
Saturday's Child	95
Silver Moon	95
Staara	50
State Street Collection	51
Steve Starr Studios	96
Studio Sew Sew	105
Studio V	51
Sugar Magnolia	53
The Sweden Shop	110

T

Thomas Moore's Men's Clothing	119
Thomas Moore's Formal Wear	119
Toshiro	97
Toys Et Cetera	115
Traffick	98

U

Ultimo	56
Underthings	99

W

Wheel & Deal	100
Whispers Lingerie	101
Wild Goose Chase Quilt Gallery	106

Y

The Yeshe Collection	57

BEVERLY HILLS CAFE

312 W Randolph / 60606   782-3355
Hours: Mon–Sat 11 am–10 pm
CC: A, C, D, M, V

If you want to settle down with a friend for a good long talk against a background of soft piano music and song, try this attractive room with its many tables and comfortable chairs. On any night it is crowded, mostly with people who work in offices in the area, but it remains surprisingly low-key and restful. Drinks cost $2 to $3.50. –AT

JOE SEGAL'S JAZZ SHOWCASE

636 S Michigan / 60605   427-4300
Hours: Fri & Sat: Extra set at 1 am, Sun: Sets at 9 &
11 pm

Any list of Chicago institutions would be incomplete without Joe Segal's. Mention him to any musician or jazzophile and you'll get an instant positive response because for forty years Joe has used his club as a showcase for the best and widest range of jazz artists, local, national and international. Count Basie is among the many who have played here, as are Stan Kenton, Maynard Ferguson and McCoy Tyner. Here it is jazz concert-style, for the aficionado, to be carefully listened to and savored.

The Showcase's present quarters are a sophisticated room just inside the lobby of the Blackstone Hotel. A cover of $8 to $12 will buy you a seat and, unlike many similar rooms, there is no drink minimum. The emphasis is on what Joe calls "American Classical Music". Among the musicians who play here regularly are Bud Freeman, Ira Sullivan, Eddie "Lockjaw" Davis, Phil Woods and Jack DeJohnette: jazz heavies who prefer attentive audiences.

Oversized blowups of photographs of Duke Ellington and Charlie Parker adorn the walls, along with a number of smaller photographs from Joe's enormous collection of pictures of musicians who have played for the Showcase over the years. The chairs are comfortable, with small tables, so that listeners can hear two or three sets with ease. Joe is always there, and he is always accessible. He likes to talk to anyone who shares his lifelong passion for jazz. And drinks are a reasonable $2 to $3.50. –AT

MOOSEHEAD BAR AND GRILL

163 W Harrison / 60605 922-3640
Reservations 922-3276
Bar & Restaurant Hours: Mon–Thurs 11 am–Midnight, Fri 11 am–2 am, Sat Noon–3 am, Sun Noon–7 pm
Entertainment: Mon, Tues, Thurs 5 pm–8:30 pm, Wed 5 pm–9:30 pm, Fri 5 pm–10 pm, Sat 9 pm–1:30 am, Sun 2 pm–5 pm
CC: A, D, M, V

Once there were three friends who liked listening to jazz so much that they opened their own jazz club and restaurant/bar. Located in Printer's Row, this is a casual room, the perfect place to relax after a hard day or a hard week—the food and drink are good and fine jazz is played live every night. We were there on Monday evening, which is Latin Jazz Night, and were well taken care of by the friendly bartender and by Joe

Edgington, one of the owners. Joe is a trumpet player himself as well as a businessman.

Joe and his partners, Roger Wolf and Bill Leininweber are all businessmen as well as jazz fanatics. Four years ago they started a jazz club which met once a month to hear Eddy Johnson play. However, once a month was not enough for them, so in 1984 they opened Moosehead—one of the few rooms in Chicago started with music in mind first and the restaurant and bar second.

The entertainment schedule changes every four weeks; there is a fixed format on certain nights. Monday is Latin Jazz, Tuesday Eddy Johnson plays, Wednesday is Big Band Night, and on Sunday afternoons you can enjoy a brunch jam session with people like Ed Thigpen, John Thadus and the Eddy DeHass Trio. So come and spend your day of rest at Moosehead. If you call before you come, you will hear a tape telling you who is playing on any particular day. Except for Mondays and Wednesdays, you can be sure you'll hear straight-ahead jazz played by musicians from all over the city.

Since different kinds of people love jazz, you'll find all sorts at Moosehead—businesspeople, construction workers from local sites, young runners from the nearby Board of Trade—they all come. And a woman can come here alone and be perfectly comfortable. It is definitely not a pick-up scene.

The decor is interesting too. An astounding collection of memorabilia covers the walls, much of it from Roger's personal collection. The bar's namesake, an enormous moosehead, is mounted over the bar. There are other mounted animal heads on the walls, along with a very old set of golf clubs, some antique skis and saddles, and an old megaphone. There are old photos, too: a gigantic one of Mayor Daley, some of almost all the U.S. Presidents, boxing champions, and Edward when he was Prince of Wales. There is also an interesting old map of Chicago.

Moosehead's answer to video games is from Riverview Park: three antique games—the crane, the eagle striker and a boxing machine—all in working condition.

This is a pleasant, convivial atmosphere. There's plenty of free parking, no cover on Sundays, Mondays and Tuesdays, and drinks run from $2 to $3.50. –AT

ANDY'S

11 E Hubbard / 60611   642-6805
Hours: Mon–Fri 11 am–10 pm, Sat 6 pm–2 pm
Entertainment: Tues–Fri 12 pm–2:30 pm, 5 pm–8 pm,
Sat 9 pm–1 am
CC: A, D, M, V

If you like live jazz, but you don't want to stay up late, get to know Andy's, the only restaurant-bar in town which offers live jazz at noon, in addition to the standard evening sessions. Jazz has been featured here since 1978 in a casual, friendly atmosphere. The owners, Scott Chisholm and Dick Goodman rely on Penny Tyler, who used to run daytime jazz concerts at Marina City, has been president of the Jazz Institute, chair of the Jazz Festival and a panel member of the Great Lakes Art Alliance, to book the jazz here. Dick runs the kitchen (there is a large selection of moderately priced dishes) and Scott Chisholm handles the business end of things. Many of the city's best-known musicians have done gigs a Andy's: people like Jim Beebe , Eddie Johnson, Barrett Deems, John Defauw, and even Dale Clevinger of the Chicago Symphony has blown his horn here. During most of the week mainstream jazz is played. But on Monday nights a 7-piece Dixieland band plays up a storm Chicago style, to chase the blues away. The same bands play week to week every night but Saturday, with musicians rotating, and each week a different group plays the noon gigs. There is no cover at noon and a nominal cover charge at night. A scene from John Belushi's *Continental Divide* was shot at Andy's; the film people left as a momento a neon sign which says

"Wall of Fame." Around it Penny has hung photos of the musicians who have performed here over the years.

Andy's customers come from every walk of life, but a typical weekday crowd includes people who work in the Loop and the Michigan Avenue area, and tourists. If you want to liven your lunch hour, or just enjoy good jazz in a relaxed setting, this is the place for you. –AT

BLUE CHICAGO

937 N State / 60610   642-6261
Hours: Mon–Thurs 8 pm–2 am, Sat 8 pm–3 am
CC: Cash Only

This hot new blues club is located just south of the Michigan Avenue Gold Coast area with its hotels and restaurants. It is a picture of spare elegance, with mauve walls and gray carpeting and the music is as good as anything in the more honky-tonk places on the North and South sides. The night we went, we heard the Phil Guys Blues Band wailing such favorites as "Red Rooster" and "Sweet Home Chicago." The dance floor is the biggest I've seen in any blues club and it was filled with people enjoying themselves. We danced until 1 am, when things seemed to be just warming up. In the coming months featured bands will be Sunnyland Slim, Bobby Dixon and the Blues Merchants, and Gloria Hardiman. The music starts at 9, and covers range from $3 to $5, depending on the night and the band. –JJ

DIXIE BAR & GRILL

225 W Chicago / 60610   642-3336
Dining Hours: Mon–Sat 11:30 am–2:30 pm,
5:30 pm–11 pm, Sun 11:30 am–3 pm, 5:30 pm–10 pm
Entertainment: Mon–Sat 8 pm–12:30 am, Sun 11:30
am–3 pm
CC: A, C, D, M, V

They're whistling Dixie here, and folks are flocking to join them. This very new fun spot serves food Louisiana Cajun style. The decor is effective: rattan furniture, pastel palm trees and stuffed fish against soft chic Deco. The idea is that you feel as though you're sitting on a porch in Bayou country, or lounging in New Orleans elegance. Either way, you can sip a mint julep for $2.75, a Dixie or Lone Star beer for $1.50, or toss off a Cajun martini for $3.00.

Music is live here from 8 to 12:30 six nights a week and during Sunday brunches. You pay a dollar apiece, collected at the table, for this treat. Dixie's affable, energetic owner, Roger Greenfield, says he plans for the musical choice to be eclectic. At this writing, you can hear, among other acts and depending on the night, Stardust—a female trio singing Andrews Sisters songs—Chuck Hedges—a nationally known clarinetist—Made in Brazil, Joe Zack's 10-piece Big Band, and the Warren Kime Jazz Quintet.

Roger emphasizes that this is a restaurant with delicious New Orleans food, but it is also a place to meet your friends, have a drink and generally enjoy yourself. If you're not too hungry, check out the oyster bar. Oysters are great with juleps. –JJ

EXIT

1653 N Wells / 60614   440-0535
Hours: Daily 8 pm–4 am, Sat 8 pm–5 am
CC: Cash Only

Complete with prom dresses, leather jackets, whips, chains and Mohawk hairdos, the regulars fill this black-painted punk club, dancing in the back or sitting and watching the video screen. The practice of slam dancing (jumping off a dance platform into the crowd) is mercifully out of style now, so the club is relatively tame. Exit has the newest music and videos in the punk and new wave scene. You can always find a place to sit and watch the strobe lights if you don't want to dance. Or you can sit and chat at the large bar in the front of the club. There is a cover on Friday and Saturday nights. Entertainment begins at 10:55. –MC

GEORGE'S

230 W Kinzie / 60610   644-2290
Hours: Mon–Thurs 5:30 pm–1 am, Fri, Sat 5:30 pm–2 am
Entertainment: Mon 9 pm, Tues–Thurs 10 pm, Fri, Sat 10 pm, 11:45 pm, Closed Sun
CC: A, M, V

On a dank, Nelson Algren kind of street nestled against the back side of the Merchandise Mart you will find this popular home of some of the best jazz and Northern Italian cuisine in town. The decor is minimalist elegant: cool grays, black marble and recessed lighting. You can't help feeling chic in this setting. Tastefulness aside, owner George Badonsky is serious about jazz, and his club offers good jazz, both domestic and international, Tuesday through Saturday. Mainstream jazz is the staple but sometimes progressive jazz, fusion and even 60's pop is thrown into the line-up. Recent groups have included Monty Alexander, Ahmad Jamal, Ray Brown, Herb Ellis, Michel Petrucciani and the Four Freshmen. The night we were there, Michel Petrucciani was playing exquisite, high-energy piano, slipping occasionally into rich George Winston lyricism. Cover for that show was $9, but it can start at $8 and climb as high as $15. Drink prices are around $3, and there is a two-drink minimum. The weekend shows start at 10 and 11:45; seating for the early cabaret dinner show is between 8 and 8:30, allowing a leisurely dinner before the kitchen closes at 9. The manager, Mike Pucci, strongly recommends making reservations; he says the second show is a better buy than the first because it is not as popular and the bands tend generally to play a little longer than the standard hour. You should call ahead also because jazz is seasonal at George's, running roughly from March to June, and from September to January. In the intervals the club is still popular for its food which is really delicious and priced to fit different pockets. There is a wide selection of hot and cold appetizers—prosciutto and kiwi, and oysters baked in asiago cheese, for instance, perfect for nibbling through the evening (from $2.75 to $6.). Dinner ($10 to $17) is available from 5:30 to 8, after which a short menu is provided. George's is good for lunch, too, or after-work drinks, but there is no live jazz 'till 10 pm.

Finally, I should mention the terrific wine list. In addition to the score or so of fine French and California wines, there are over 100 Italian wines. And if you're celebrating something—and George's seems to exist for such occasions—you shouldn't miss choosing from among the 22 sparkling wines and champagnes. Valet parking is available. -JJ

GET ME HIGH LOUNGE

1758 N Honore / 60622   278-8154
Hours: Bar, 3 pm–2 am daily, Sat 'til 3 am
Entertainment: 9:30 pm nightly, Live Jazz, Sat early set 7 pm, Sun afternoon: Vocal workshop
CC: Cash Only

"Sophisticated" and "elegant" are not the words for this small corner bar. "Arty" and "down-home" come closer to it. Anyway, to get the real feel of this lounge, you must stop by for a drink one night. The walls are covered with attractive graffiti, done by some of the many artists who hang out here. Various bands play excellent jazz and there is no cover. The entrance to the bathrooms and the cigarette machine is off the small stage, right next to where the musicians play! -AT

LIMELIGHT

632 N Dearborn / 60610   337-2985
Hours: Daily, 9 pm–4 am
CC: A ($15 min)

It was a New Yorker—self-made millionaire Peter Gatien—who took the old Chicago Historical Society building and turned it into an enormous, chic nightclub, like the chic nightclubs he has already opened in other cities, including London and New York. Gatien, who cuts an eerie figure, with shoulder-length locks and a black eyepatch, has a flair for creating a completely modern space and retaining the charm and detail of the older building that houses it. In the Limelight foyer you will see, in a large glass case, a mermaid with her lower half swung over the arm of a chair, reading a bestseller. There are other large glass cases with one or more inhabitants acting out bizarre little plays, and you can even join in if you wish. In an enormous room, with 50-foot vaulted ceiling, and muralled walls, there is plenty of seating for conversation and/or watching the eccentrically turned-out crowd. The 2,800 square foot dance floor is the most attractive in Chicago—and probably the slipperiest, thanks to the heavily polished wood. A balcony circles the floor and offers an interesting vantage point. When you're dressing to come here, bear in mind that the clientele has a completely avant garde attitude toward clothing; sneakers and jeans are not allowed. During the week, the management has started a series of fashion shows and art exhibits. The music and sound systems are phenomenal and the entire experience is well worth the $5 cover Sunday through Thursday, and $7 Friday and Saturday. Drinks range from $2.75 to $5.00. –AT

THE RACCOON CLUB

812 N Franklin / 60610   943-1928
Hours: Mon–Thurs: 5 pm–1 am, Fri & Sat 5 pm–2 am
CC: A, C, D, M, V

This cozy cabaret, in the basement of a renovated factory building, provides fine entertainment in a great atmosphere. Owner/performer Jan Hobson, who works days in the advertising department of the Continental Bank, really knows how to throw a party. There is a comfortable Deco atmosphere and a small selection of delicious food: finger sandwiches and paté and Raccoon Club brownies. Seven years ago Jan formed a group called Jan Hobson and her Bad Review. Backed up by a male singer, drums and a piano, Jan sings marvelous songs from the '20s and '30s. She started the Club so that she could have a good room for regular performances, and she does her own smashing Saturday nights gigs and also books top acts for the tiny stage.

There is no seating at the bar, but if you are alone they will seat you any weeknight and even on weekends, if they possibly can. There is jazz at least two nights a week, a spirited musical mix on other nights and The Bad Review on Saturday playing to SRO crowds. There is a nominal nightly cover charge and reservations are recommended on Saturday. It might be wise to call on other nights, because the situation can change. There is no dress code, but you should be aware that people come here gussied up in everything from feather boas and sequins to tuxedos complete with cummerbunds. Jan herself wears fabulous vintage gowns from Silver Moon and Studio V. All sorts of people come to the Club, and the atmosphere varies. But everyone enjoys the music. So stop by for a set or two of The Bad Review. You'll be glad you did. –AT

RENDEZVOUS

1400 N Lake Shore Dr / 60610   280-8800
Entertainment: Daily, 8 pm–1 am
CC: D, M, V

This beautifully understated room harks back to the 1950s, the days when classy piano lounges provided the best night life in town. The Rendezvous is just down the hall from Arturo's Coq Au Vin in one of the loveliest old buildings in the city. It has an intimate atmosphere and fine entertainment—it's especially pleasant to have a nightcap while James Lewis plays jazz piano and sings. –AT

YVETTE

1206 N State / 60610   280-1700
Hours: Food: 11:30 am–1:30 am, Sat 'til 2:30 am
Music starts about 8 nightly
CC: A, D, V

With its live jazz and pop piano music, and subdued gray Deco decor, Yvette is easily the most sophisticated, upscale night spot in the Rush Street area. The clientele is a mix of all ages in pinstripe and silk, and most nights there's a feeling of money and singles intrigue in the air. This is a small club, popular because of its location and its nightly no-cover music, and patrons are often packed in like riders on a rush hour El train. Drinks are moderately priced at $2.50 to $3.50. When the weather is nice, Yvette pulls aside the front windows, and you can have a meal or a drink, listen to the music, and watch the passing Rush Street scene. (JJ)

ZANIE'S COMEDY CLUB

1548 N Wells / 60610   337-4027
Hours: No shows/No bar service. Wed, Thurs, Sun Shows

at 8:30 pm
Fri Shows at 9 pm & 11:15 pm, Sat 7 pm, 9 pm, 11:15 pm
CC: M, V

For an $8 or $9 cover and a two-drink minimum, you can watch three or four stand-up comedians perform in one evening in this popular spot. Some of these comedians are nationally known; some are local. The routines vary from extremely dirty to refreshingly clean. Pete Fogel and Bobby Collins appear frequently, as does Skip Groparis, who has an excellent, refreshingly clean act which includes a great impression of John Lennon. Marsha Wakefield, a popular black comedienne, will be appearing here often. Reservations are a must, but even with reservations it's important to come early so that you can sit near the stage. –MC

ARTFUL DODGER

1734 W Wabansia / 60622   227-6859
Hours: Tues–Sun 5 pm–2 am, Sat 8 pm–3 am,
Entertainment: 10 pm–closing

If you can manage to find this underground artists' hangout (and I'll help you: Wabansia is an east-west street, and it is 1700 North) you're in for an evening of strange comings and goings by some of the most interesting and/or interesting-looking people inside the city limits. The atmosphere is smoke-filled and arty (the walls are covered with local masterpieces), and various creative folk mingle, drink and dance to widely different kinds of music, from blues to '50s rock and roll. There's never a cover and drinks average about $2.00. –AT

BERLIN

954 W Belmont / 60657   348-4975
Hours: Daily 4 pm–4 am, Sat 'til 5 am
CC: Cash Only

Chicago Magazine gave this bar an award for the most creative use of video in a dance club. But there's lots more than video entertainment here. On Tuesday nights at 10:30 there are male strippers, and male and female wrestlers appear frequently on week nights. Charity O'Day, a favorite at Berlin, is a burlesque stripper from the '40s who still uses her tassles. On some nights Roberta Rubenstein plays the accordian. There are Japanese nights, and on Sunday nights owners Shirley Mooney and Tim Sullivan serve pizza and show a surprise feature movie. On Thursdays, beginning at 5:30 pm Berlin shows the previous week's *All My Children* episodes without commercials. If you want to stay on, you can join the regular Thursday night crowd that orders out for dinner. On Fridays and Saturdays there is a $1.00 cover charge. Clientele is an interesting mixture of gays and straights. Have fun. –MC

B.L.U.E.S.

2519 N Halsted / 60614   528-1012
Hours: Daily 8 pm, Sunday 5 pm, Sunday 9 pm show
CC: Cash Only

In this cramped little bar, Chicago's most notable blues stars perform, even on their off nights, for the neighborhood audience and for each other. To mention a few who play here: Sugar Blues, John Watkins, Otis Clay, Eddie Clearwater, The Jimmy Johnson Blues Band, and Magic Slim and the Teardrops. The acoustics are bad, the air is smoky and the seating is crowded. But the entertainment is terrific. Cover prices vary, drinks are reasonably priced. B.L.U.E.S. is open 7 nights a week. The entertainment hours vary, so call first. –MC

THE BULLS

1916 N Lincoln Park West / 60614   337-3000
Hours: Daily & Weekends 8 pm–4 am, Music starts
9:30 pm
CC: A, D, M, V

This is a cave-like basement club which has an intimate feeling despite the fact that it is usually crowded.

The music is varied—everything from Brazilian combos to live jazz. For those of you who like late nights, The Bulls is less crowded after midnight when the musicians are really wound up. The cover charge is $2.50 Sunday thru Thursday and $4.00 Friday and Saturday and drinks are reasonable. The large menu includes nachos, sandwiches, salads and rich desserts. But music is the main attraction. Check *The Reader* or call for billings. -MC

CROSS CURRENTS

3206 N Wilton / 60657   472-7884
Call ahead for hours & entertainment schedule.
Bar: 5 pm–2 am Daily, Entertainment: Tues 8 pm, Fri 9 pm, Sat. 7 pm, 9 pm, 11 pm, Sun 7 pm
M-W-T Special Events

This pretty cabaret features comedy, experimental acts and music. The jazz is sensational. During the Happy Hour (5-7 weekdays) snacks are free and the atmosphere is conducive to conversation. In the summer you can drink outside on the front patio. Upstairs owner John Economos gives occasional Latin dance parties featuring La Confidencia and Motown with Chicago disc jockeys as MCs. Another aspect of Cross Currents are meetings run by political activists and non-profit organizations who rent space from John for a low fee. You can hear and see Central and South American politicians, singers and musicians. Cover and drink minimums vary. -MC

DENI'S DEN RESTAURANT AND CLUB

2941 N Clark / 60614   348-8888

Hours: Wed–Sun 5 pm–4 am, Sat 'til 5 am
CC: A, M, V

This is a beautiful restaurant with whitewashed walls and a high ceiling that gives the room a clean, open feeling. Hanging plants are scattered about, and the tables arranged around the stage, are covered with white tablecloths. The owners, Christos and Georgia Verdos, came to this country from Greece in 1968. They settled first in Seattle, where they worked in various restaurants, including Seattle's first Greek restaurant. Christos had a dream of creating an eating place that provided not only authentic homemade food, but beautiful music, in a Mykonos garden setting. When they came to Chicago in 1976, the couple opened Deni's Den, where they have welcomed thousands of customers over the years.

The well-dressed patrons enjoy a night of lively entertainment and conviviality. Weekends are very busy, so you should make reservations. It's a friendly crowd: people have been known to leave here with more friends than they had when they came in. And remember the late closing for those nights when you want to do a lot of celebrating.

The cook knows his stuff, turning out delicious food at reasonable prices. But the best thing about Deni's Den is the music. Christos and Georgia work hard to get talented musicians, often flying entire groups in from Greece. Vasilis Gaitanos has been playing piano and singing here for years. His music— sometimes light, sometimes with political messages and words by writers like Garcia Lorca and Brendan Behan—always comes from the heart and can be very moving. I heard Irene Raiku, a singer who is half-

African and half-Greek, belting out sultry songs, backed by a terrific bouzouki band. The clientele, about 50% Greek, likes to dance to popular Greek tunes. Deni's Den has an international reputation as a center for Greek culture; visitors come from all over the world, including Mrs. Margaret Papandreou, Melina Mercouri and Anthony Quinn. Once Ann-Margret was among the last to leave, exhausted after dancing til 5 a.m.

Drinks are $2.50 and $2.75 before 8:15; after that they are $3 and $3.75. Imported Greek wine is $12.95 a bottle. There is no cover and no minimum. Limited parking is available in back of the restaurant—an important consideration in this part of town.

Christos and Georgia work 18 hours a day to make Deni's Den the finest place of its kind—a must if you want a taste of the best Greek traditions. –AT

JUKEBOX SATURDAY NIGHT

2251 N Lincoln / 60614   525-5000
Hours: Mon 6 pm–2 am, Tues–Thurs 8 pm–3 am, Fri 8 pm–4 am, Sat 8 pm–5 am, Closed Sun
CC: A, D

Perhaps you've seen the old Chevrolet protruding from the front of a building as you've driven down Lincoln Avenue. That building houses Jukebox Saturday Night—a multi-roomed club where '50s and '60s pop music plays into the wee hours. If you don't want to jitterbug, you can enjoy the music and the ornaments that go back to the '30s. The disk jockey, who is happy to take your requests, sits in a hot rod. Old juke boxes decorate the bar, as do dunk tanks from the old Riverview amusement park. You can watch movie classics on the large TV screens but you won't be able to hear a word in this noisy bar. However, despite minor inconveniences, everyone has a good time. The cover is $2 weekdays and $3 on weekends. Drinks are moderately priced.

The owner, Jim Rittenberg, has recently installed a Talking Alcohol Breath Analyzer video machine. For 50¢ this machine will tell you the alcohol level in your blood, and if it is too high will make suggestions— mainly that you do not drive. Jim's goal is to save lives. Wait 10 or 15 minutes after your last drink and then use the machine. You may be surprised. -MC

THE LATIN VILLAGE

2528 N Lincoln / 60614   472-6166
Hours: Mon, Wed, Fri, Sun, 7 pm–4 am, Sat 7 pm–5 am, Closed Tues & Thurs
CC: Cash Only

This popular dance spot features salsa orchestras such as La Confidencia and Los Merecumbre. The music starts at 10 pm so if you want a table, arrive before then on weekends. It is fun to sit or stand at the bar and sample the strong but delicious cocktails. Be sure to get dressed up because jeans or other casual attire are forbidden. There is a cover of $5 on weekends and a 2 drink minimum at the tables. -MC

MEDUSA'S

3257 N Sheffield / 60657   549-9212
Hours: Fri & Sat Only, 6:30 pm–11 pm, Midnight–Dawn

Aptly called "the Limelight of the Masses" by *Chicago Magazine*, this dance club serves no alcohol but has lots of juices. This is probably a good thing since the very young crowd - 18 to low 20s - gets pretty sweaty in the course of a Friday or Saturday night, the only two nights the club is open. The place gets really mobbed and you'll find long lines waiting to get in.

On Saturday nights there's a teen dance segment (6:30-11:00 pm) after which everyone is asked to leave and the doors are closed until midnight, then reopened and everyone is carded to make sure he or she is at least 18. Once in you can dance 'til dawn.

Housed in a converted apartment building, the main floor is for dancing, the second floor, with balcony, features glass enclosures in which little dramas are played out, while the third floor has several dozen/ large video displays sufficient to fill the hungriest eye.

Although a disk jockey spins out the new wave music most of the time, there are occasional live band performances. –MC & AT

NEO

2350 N Clark / 60614   528-2622
Hours: Nightly, 9 pm-4 am
CC: Cash Only.

This used to be a punk bar; now it is basically a dance club for people whose only concern is having a good time. The music is a combination of new wave, punk, top forty and popular disco. Any kind of clothing goes here, from Perry Ellis silk blouses to strapless prom dresses, but by and large the crowd (Lincoln Parkers, suburbanites) is well-dressed. The dance floor is surrounded by video screens and you can watch the screens or the dance floor from any corner of the club. Everyone dances with a partner. The dancing gets hot at 11 at the earliest on week nights and somewhat later on weekends. Women can come alone and feel comfortable; people are concentrating on the music. A disc jockey will take your requests, and the staff are friendly. Drinks are about $3.00 and on weekends there is a $2 to $3 cover. Neo is not home to youth only, incidentally; all ages can be seen here on any given night. –MC & AT

THE 950 CLUB—"LUCKY NUMBER"

950 W Wrightwood / 60614   929-8955
929-1191: for A.E. feature information only
CC: Cash Only

In this avant garde night spot, you can hear music you won't hear elsewhere in the city. Under the management of Noe (pronounced Noah) Boudreau it has become one of Chicago's most popular bars, where you will find the latest imported tapes and videos. On Japanese Music Night, for instance, you can dress in a kimono and dance to wild, exotic sounds. On other nights features have been the music of The Cure, the music of Lou Reed, Roxy Music, David Bowie and Talking Heads. The clientele is a mixture of very young and middling older, all sharing open attitudes toward music. This is a cosmopolitan, innovative club with an international flavor, Prices are reasonable and the atmosphere is friendly. The 2 for 1 drink specials more than make up for the small cover charge on special events nights. –MC

THE OCTAGON PUB

2483 N Clark / 60614   549-1132
Hours: Mon–Fri 2 pm–2 am, Sat 12 pm–3 am,
Sun 12 pm–2 am
CC: Cash Only

In this pleasant neighborhood bar the dance floor is large, the sound system is fabulous, and the music ranges from new wave and punk to top forty tunes. It's a nice place to go after work because it is not a crowded singles bar; it appeals to people who like contemporary music but are not comfortable with the frenetic atmosphere of punk bars. The staff are pleasant and obliging, there is no cover or minimum and the drinks are reasonably priced. –MC

OZ

2917 N Sheffield / 60657   975-8100
Serving hours: Sun–Fri 4 pm–2 am, Sat 4 pm–3 am
Entertainment: Thurs & Fri 9:30 pm, Sat 10 pm
CC: A, M, V

This is a sophisticated club with fine food and drink and great live jazz entertainment. The decor is slick and attractive and the lighting and sound systems are perfect. In summer there is a beer garden.

Among the groups which play at Oz are the Joan Hickey Quartet with a terrific young jazz singer named Suzanne Palmer, who sings Billie Holiday and Nancy Wilson songs with tremendous stage presence; then there is the Joel Spencer Trio, a popular jazz ensemble. This is a relatively new club and the owner is still experimenting, so bands will change often. Call

Oz for the weekly schedule. The clientele, by the way, are devoted jazz buffs who tend to become testy if talk goes on during the sets.

Ron Schoenstadt, the owner, has had a lot of experience in the food business as a waiter at George's, Printers Row Restaurant, Eugene's and Gene Sage's. In the '60s he was a civil rights photographer; several of his award-winning photographs appeared in *Life* magazine. If you are lucky you might see Ron wearing his "I am a jazz impressario" outfit, consisting of beret, cigarette holder, Sun glasses, Hawaiian shirt and Panama trousers.

Oz specializes in cognac and armagnac, and lays claim to the finest assortment of brandies in town. The price for an ounce to an ounce and a half ranges from $3.75 to $55. There is a full bar service, of course, if you prefer cocktails or beer. Prices are relatively high and there is a $3 cover charge for entertainment.

Some specialized foods—pastas and salads—are being planned. –AT

PARADISE

2856 N Broadway / 60657   871-4200
Bar: Daily 3 pm–4 am
Entertainment: Mon, Thurs, Fri, 10 pm–4 am, Wed
10:30 pm–4 am, Sat 10 pm–5 am, Tues and Sun
Ballroom closed
CC: Cash Only

There are four different rooms here: a ballroom, the Lounge for quiet conversations and private parties, a jazz room and a night club theatre. Bob Fischer, the club's promotional manager, has turned this once run-down spot into a center for all kinds of interesting entertainment. Call, if you want to find out just when the body builders or the string quartet will appear. Or you can dance the salsa or watch Bob do body paintings in the Blue Zebra Lounge. Note that hours vary. –MC

PARK WEST VIDEO DANCE PARTY

322 W Armitage / 60614   929-5959
Hours: Saturdays only: 9:30 pm–2 am
Other special video dance nights. Call for information.
CC: A, D, M (Drinks only)

Here, once a week only, is your chance to mix and mingle with Chicago sophisticates—and of course dance with them on a stage otherwise used by top concert performers. Lights cascade in an astounding variety of colors, and there are larger-than-life video screens which display the music and images of American pop culture. Cover is $7 and drinks run from $2 to $3.50. –AT

POPS FOR CHAMPAGNE

2934 N Sheffield / 60657   472-1000
Hours: Daily, 5 pm–2 am, Sun 3 pm–2 am
CC: A, C, D, M, V

This is basically a champagne bar, although you can get mixed drinks here, too, which run about $5, along with light appetizers and cheesecake. Tom and Linda Verhey have modeled Pops after a champagne bar which Tom visited in Vienna. The decor is pleasant with soft lighting, old posters, a bar made of wood from old mantelpieces. There are booths in back and a cozy working fireplace. In summer you can sip your drinks in the back garden. And wherever you sit you can listen to good jazz on tape.

The champagnes are vintage, non-vintage and rosé at various prices. The staff will help you select from 17 champagnes sold by the glass. Allow about $4 or $5 and up for sparkling wines per glass. Or you may order a bottle for as little as $20. For $49 a bottle, there is the Deutz Cuveés William, slightly bitter, or at $75 Taittinger Comtes Blanc de Blanc, one of Tom's favorites. You might want to splurge some evening with a group of friends and order the Laurent Perrier Grand Siécle 1975 for $59.

Pops' clientele is a mixture of young professionals, theatre people and suburbanites. Among the local celebrities seen here in the evenings, or at the winter Sunday afternoon jazz concerts, the summer musical festivals and the frequent champagne-tasting parties, are Mike Royko and Mary Ann Childers. Pops is not a singles bar, by the way, so women can be comfortable coming here alone. –MC

RAINBO CLUB

1150 N Damen / 60622   489-5999
Hours: Mon–Fri 4 pm–2 am, Sat 8 pm–3 am,
Sun 8 pm–2 am
CC: Cash Only

This bar attracts a large crowd of writers, artists,

musicians and neighborhood folk. Although owner Gavin Morrison had done some minor remodeling, the Rainbo Club looks basically as it did when Nelson Algren wrote about it in *The Man With The Golden Arm*. The walls are covered with work by Chicago artists and photographers. A talent night will be a regular feature, so call and tell Gavin about your rare skills and you might have a chance to perform. Gavin has installed an old photo booth and for $1 you and your date can strike four poses. The bar is large and comfortable, the drinks are reasonably priced and the the music is especially good because Gavin plays his own tapes—reggae, new music, Japanese music and jazz. Dancing is encouraged—the club has a floor that is big enough for it. Nelson Algren lived a block from the club, on Evergreen Street. -MC

THE ROXY

1505 W Fullerton / 60614   472-8100
Hours: 11:30 am–2 am Daily, Sat 'til 3 am
CC: Cash or Check Only

This friendly cabaret with unusual entertainment used to be at Wrightwood and Racine, but was forced to close when Pat and Betty Murray lost their lease. Fortunately it has opened again, now with two rooms to avoid the old controversies between music lovers and conversationalists. You can now enjoy music in the music room and eat and chat in the restaurant. Entertainment includes comedy, jazz, folk, pop, country and blues. From time to time 16 millimeter movies are shown; the seats come from the old Biograph Theatre.

Although nationally known groups like the Dooley brothers play the Roxy, on most nights the entertainers are local. Some talent is discovered during the Thursday "open mike" nights.

The Murrays collect movie memorabilia. There are lots of old movie posters on the walls, including some rare ones advertising Marilyn Monroe movies. The entire bar top is a collage of pictures of movie stars mixed with photographs of The Roxy's regular customers.

The Roxy opens for lunch at 11:30. There is a large selection of sandwiches and salads and the hamburgers are award-winning.

During Happy Hour, drinks are $1. In the music room the cover varies from $3 to $5 depending on the act. Entertainment starts at 9 pm.

Facets Multimedia is just down the street. You might want to go to a movie there and then drop in at The Roxy. Or try calling ahead to see if the Murrays are showing a movie that night and spend the evening there. Dinner, movies, music and drinks. You can't beat it. −MC

THE VIC THEATRE

3145 N Sheffield / 60657   472-0366
Box Office: Mon–Sat 12 pm–6 pm
Call for hours and schedules.
CC: A, M, V, Ticketron Box Office

This is one of Chicago's newest entertainment houses, set in one of the oldest and most beautifully refurbished vaudeville theatres in town. You can see performers from Cleo Laine to Spyro Gira in a cabaret setting unequaled in its attention to detail, from the state-of-the-art sound system to the polished brass railings lining the seating perimeter. The owners, Tom and Walter Klein, are experimenting with acts here, and part of the fun is not knowing what to expect. Sometimes there are all-ages dance parties where the front row tables are cleared away and dancers move to the music of Joan Jett or the Violent Femmes. For a more sedate evening, come when Chick Correa or Wynton Marsalis are doing their thing. I attended a fabulous Sarah Vaughan concert here with a quiet, mature audience. People were very dressed up that evening, but it's okay to come here dressed casually. Country and Western, '50s Rock 'n' Roll, Heavy Metal and comedy all have their nights. In fact, this is where Second City held its own 25th anniversary celebration, a star-studded evening captured on tape by HBO. The Vic is developing a national reputation.

Only a year or so ago the theatre was in a sad state of disrepair. It was built in 1910, and had recently been used to show first porno and then Indian films. Tom and Walter restored every inch to its original color scheme of deep blue and burgundy with gold rococo borders. The main floor has been torn out and multi-level cabaret seating installed, so the viewing is good everywhere in the room. And the atmosphere is informal. You may be seated with strangers, European-style, but it's a nice way to meet people with common musical interests. There are two bars on the first level, and one on the second. The second floor lobby is especially attractive with its vaulted ceiling and gigantic mural of Columbus landing in the

New World offering a marked contrast on any given night to the contemporary scene.

There is a two-drink minimum in addition to the price of the tickets which range from $10 to $17.50 and can be bought at the Vic box office or at any Ticketron outlet. Drinks run from $2 to $3.50.

The parking situation is terrible. The Vic's lot is too small, and the nearby streets are filled with residents' cars. The good news is that parking is scarce because the neighborhood is teeming with people enjoying the burgeoning nightlife. With Pops, Oz and Medusa all located near the Vic, there is plenty to keep you busy for many a long night of entertainment. –AT

THE VU BAR & GRILL

2624 N Lincoln / 60614   871-0205
Hours: Daily 7 am–4 am, Sun 12 pm–4 am
CC: Cash Only

The Vu has popular jazz concerts on Sunday nights when owner Dave Jemillo pulls his portable stage out of the back room and the Vu Jazz Quartet plays while various Chicago musicians sit in. The rest of the week the Vu relies on a jukebox with an unusually varied selection and an occasional appearance by Gerry Grossman, "The Human Jukebox," who can sing any tune you suggest, no matter how obscure. While you are there try a bowl of Dave's famous chili, which is only $1.50. Sandwiches are reasonably priced too, and there are drink specials almost every day. Call to find out about them and to find out when the Vu will be having the next Motown Dance Party. –MC

WEST END

1170 W Armitage / 60614   525-0808
Hours: Mon–Sat 7 pm–2 am
CC: Cash Only

This looks like a typical neighborhood tavern until after 10 pm. Then the audience and the stage start to jump. The West End is a center for new music and books, avant-garde pop, new wave and rock bands. The emphasis is on innovation, not nostalgia. One new trend is "garage punk" rooted in the '60s. Most of the musicians who play it come from Boston. The result is a noisy but interesting place filled with young people. Cover ranges from $2 to $7. Drinks are reasonable and there is no minimum. Beer costs between $1 and $2.25. –MC

THE WILD HARE AND SINGING ARMADILLO FROG SANCTUARY

3530 N Clark / 60657   327-0800
Hours: Daily, 8 pm–2 am, Sat 'til 3 am, Music starts 10 pm
CC: Cash Only

This club is the center for reggae music in the Midwest and it is Chicago's oldest and most popular reggae dance club. The best of local and imported Jamaican and Ethiopian bands play here. It is the same kind of music you hear in Jamaica. I have enjoyed Debby DeFire, Michael Black and the Dreads and Safari. Yabba Griffith plays here, and Traxx and Inity, featuring Devon Brown.

The clientele is mixed—university students, Africans in native costume, recent Jamaican immigrants,

well-dressed Gold Coasters. The owners opened the
bar in 1979, intending it to be multi-racial and to in-
troduce reggae music to Chicago. Posters of reggae
stars, foreign and domestic, cover the walls. Bob Mar-
ley's widow Rita stops by whenever she is in Chicago.
So does Jimmy Cliff.

Weekends are crowded, and everyone dances.
Watch *The Reader* for the schedule of groups. –MC

ASI ES COLOMBIA

3910 N Lincoln / 60613   348-7444
Hours: Wed & Fri 7 pm–2 am, Sat 7 pm–3 am
CC: Cash Only

This is a large, traditional Latin night club. The clientele is mostly Spanish-speaking, but the waitresses all speak English. The large orchestras play a variety of popular Latin music. If you don't want to dance the cumbria or the salsa, you can sit back and watch the accomplished dancers on the floor really getting into it.

Owner Fabio Barrero was born in Colombia and has managed restaurants and clubs in both Chicago and New York. Consequently, his club is for the most part smoothly run. There are delicious snacks (broasted chicken, nachos and *chorizos* or sausages) but the portions are small and service is slow, so you shouldn't count on them to replace dinner.

The main attraction here is music and dancing. There are excellent local bands like the Combo Combo Colombia and Nueva Dimensión. If you call before you come,, you can find out what kind of music to expect. If you arrive before 9 you will probably get a table right away, but if you like to go out late, you will probably have to wait at least half an hour.

Drinks are moderately priced. There is a cover charge of between $3 and $5 but no drink minimum. It is a club policy to request than men wear jackets although they are not required. –MC

BIDDY MULLIGANS

7644 N Sheridan Rd / 60626   761-6532

Hours: Mon, Wed, Thurs 8 pm–2 am, Fri & Sat 'til 3 am, Closed Sun & Tues
CC: Cash Only

This blues club is named after an Irish prohibitionist who was so unpopular in Ireland that bars were named for her out of spite. Incredibly the owners, since 1981, are Shamsuddin V. Lahka and Shamsuddin A Khowaja, brothers-in-law from Pakistan, who bought the club as a business venture but who have become dedicated blues buffs. Talk to them about the history of Chicago blues and the present blues scene and you'll see.

On Mondays, Biddy features reggae and sometimes rock on Wednesdays. But the rest of the time blues is the main attraction—groups like Otis Clay, Junior Wells, the Son Seals Band and Clarence "Gatemouth" Brown and many others. Check the *Reader* to find out the schedule.

The entertainment begins around 10 pm. It's best to get there early, especially on weekends because people come from nearby Loyola and Northwestern Universities and, in fact, from all over the Midwest, to enjoy the blues. The dance floor is excruciatingly small, but people are polite and you can eventually attain more space.

Dress is casual and drinks are $1.75 and $2.75. The cover is $2 to $5 except when the Sams turn the bar over to a charity benefit, when it can go as high as $6 or $7. –MC

CAFE CONTINENTAL

5515 N Lincoln / 60625   878-7077

*Hours: Tues–Sun 5 pm–4 am, Sat 5 pm–5 am, Closed Mon
Entertainment: 8:30 & 10:30 pm
CC: A, C, D, M, V*

This club, which has just been remodeled, offers food, live entertainment and dancing six nights a week. Owners Robert and Anna Stulac, brother and sister, are from Croatia, and the Continental has a definite middle European atmosphere. The specialties on the menu reflect this (although you can also order standard American fare), as does the floor show, which features a glamourous blonde Yugoslavian singer who gives her ethnic audience its favorite songs. Eddy, the master of ceremonies, sings and tells off-color jokes. He was not our cup of tea, but since his stories are in various languages, you may be fortunate enough not to understand them.

The floor show lasts about 45 minutes and then everybody gets back to dancing. The night we were there the band played "Spanish Eyes", "Don't Cry for Me, Argentina", "Arrivederci Roma", "The Anniversary Waltz", a chachacha and several pop songs—all in one set. This presented no problem to the expert dancers who crowd the floor and we were steered politely by our partners, none of whom spoke English. There are no wallflowers at this night club—so come with your dancing shoes on!

The female clientele before midnight sport bouffant hairdos and chiffon cocktail dresses, with a sprinkling of skin-tight leather pants, mini skirts and 5 inch heels. After midnight a generally younger singles group takes over—Robert and Anna themselves are in their early 20s—and the place becomes more Ameri-

175

can. So come early if you want to catch the ethnic flavor.

This is a very large, attractive Art Deco room and there are no bad tables. Robert or Anna will seat you and send the waitress over immediately. Usually reservations are not necessary. –MC

CHICAGO COMEDY SHOWCASE

1943 W Irving Park / 60614   348-1101
Hours: Thurs 8 pm, Fri–Sat 8 pm & 10 pm
CC: Cash Only

Jim Shey, the owner of the Showcase, worked several years ago at the Quicksilver Theatre Company. When it closed he and several other actors decided to open their on comedy club, and Chicago Comedy Showcase is the result.

If you hang in there you will see some of the city's funniest entertainment. There are comedy teams, ventriloquists, improvisational groups, magicians, and the inevitable stand-up comic. Some of the performers are veterans who have appeared on TV—on the David Letterman Show, for instance. Others are virtual novices. People come long distances to see these shows; much of the audience are regulars who come once or twice a month.

On Friday and Saturday the Chicago Comedy Review, an amusing improvisational group, performs at 7 pm. At 9 and 11 Jim's star attraction appears after the audience has been "warmed up" by stand-up comics. The night I went the star attraction was Judy Tenuta—truly one of the funniest, most original and outrageous comediennes I have ever seen. She is impossible to describe—you have to see her for yourself. But come early; she attracts crowds.

The acts that preceded Judy varied the night I was there; some were funny and smooth, but two stand-up comedians were pretty bad. Jim is aware of this; he intends to keep the club experimental, and sometimes things don't work out. But some of his best performers have been discovered on Thursday "open mike" night. Call for an audition if you're interested.

Don't be put off by the decor. Except for the gaudy bust of Elvis Presley at the entrance, the appearance of this room is decidedly no-frills. The church pews that serve as seats are decidedly hard, and the only drink available is water, which is free with the $6 cover charge. The night we were there the room was decidedly warm; we could have used a lemonade.

Nevertheless the evening was a lot of fun. Several times a year Jim Shey gives parties at the Showcase: an annual spring prom party, when customers come dressed in old prom clothes, National Gorilla Suit Day, which I leave to your imagination, and a New Years Eve Party—sold out weeks in advance—when Judy Tenuta and her accordian head a star-studded cast.

Bring your own brown paper bag if you like, and relax. You'll have a good time. -MC

COCONUTS

5246 N Broadway / 60657 878-5400
Wed–Sun 8 pm–4 am, Closed Mon & Tues
CC: Cash Only

As you might guess from the name, a visit to Coconuts will whisk you from chilly gray Chicago to a tropical paradise as quick as you can give your car to the valet.

The exterior is Caribbean pink stucco: "Coconuts" and the outlines of palm trees are emblazoned on it in blue and green neon. Inside is more neon, along with Beardsley prints and nude mannikins on the walls and in 3-D in the center of the bar. The floors are black and white tiles, there are plenty of ferns, and, naturally enough, there is a full-sized palm tree in the middle of the dance floor. It is tropical, a little campy and a little kinky and a lot of fun.

People come here to dance, and the music is eclectic and somewhat unusual, coming in loud and clear. We happened to visit the club on Halloween, so we shared the floor with dancing bears, Reagans and Nixons, belly dancers, a bumblebee and other exotic and wicked creatures. On most nights the crowd is a well-turned-out mix of locals and others. There is no cover on Wednesdays and Thursdays and it runs $3 and $5 on weekends. For special nights like Halloween it is a stiff $10. Drinks go from $1.75 to $3.25. There is a coat check and, as noted above, a car valet service. –JJ

NO EXIT

6970 N Glenwood / 60626   743-3355
Hours: Mon–Thurs 11 am–Midnight, Fri–Sun 11 am–
1 am
CC: Cash Only

This remains the homiest cafe in the city, although it has had a checkered 28-year history of owners and locations. Incidentally, the furniture is the original. Alcohol is not served: you can choose from an extensive list of coffees and teas, and the menu includes salads, sandwiches and daily specials. Breakfast is served all day.

No Exit is known for folk singing. Doug Lofstrom and Jeff Newell often appear here. Merle Boley and Hank Hirsch give jazz concerts on Sunday afternoons and classical ensembles perform on Monday nights.

People play chess, checkers and bridge here afternoons and evenings, adding to the No Exit's pub-like atmosphere. The walls are lined with shelves filled with books and games. Brian and Sue Kozin, the present owners, who met while both were working here, have a free and easy policy about lending books. You can borrow one and if you want to keep it, you can contribute another that you no longer want.

You need a relaxed attitude when you come to No Exit, because no one here is in a hurry about anything. So just enjoy the good food and home-away-from-home atmosphere. –MC

OPAL STATION

6655 N Clark / 60626   761-6685
Hours: Sun–Fri 4 pm–2 am, Sat 4 pm–3 am
Entertainment: Fri–Sat 10:30 pm & Midnight
CC: Cash Only

This is a gay and lesbian bar. Everyone else is invited, of course. Owner Ted Hoerl has a commitment to provide top entertainment in a pleasant environment for the gay community. Opal Station appears to be a success: it has been going great guns now for three years.

There are two rooms: an informal, no-cover bar room, and next to it the cabaret, where live entertainment is provided on weekends only. From the gay circuit there are Romanofsky and Phillips, folk rock musicians and comedians. From "men's movement music"—music performed by men and intended to break down female stereotypes—are Geoff Morgan, Peter Alsop and Charlie Murphy. Mary Lynn Morrison and Bill Muzillo have a classic cabaret act. Robin Flowers leads a women's bluegrass band.

Sharon Carlson and The Tea He's (Matthew Ward and Sherwood Montgomery) are hilarious singing comedy trio who also appear at the Raccoon Club. Sharon Carlson calls herself "the diva of dizziness" and describes the experience of viewing her act as one of "mystic hysteria".

The club has a theatrical atmosphere—note especially the silver lamé curtains in the cabaret. Snacks, sandwiches and daily specials are served. In the cabaret, when there is live entertainment there is a $3–$5 cover and a two-drink minimum. During the week you must rely on the juke box where the selection ranges from Cyndi Lauper to Martha and the Vandellas.

There is free parking in the back. -MC

RIVIERA

4746 N Racine / 60640   769-6300
Hours: Wed–Fri 9 pm–4 am, Sat 9 pm–5 am
CC: A, M, V

This dance club, in a renovated vaudeville theatre, has frescoes, gilt, stone carvings, a huge bar and a dance floor with the wildest light show in town. There are streaks of blue and green lasers, "double dice" lights which spin and roll and a 1,200-foot neon apparatus which simulates Times Square on New Year's Eve. Through these lights, and the smoke and the glitter on the dancer's clothes, pulses the sound of all your pop favorites. As manager Tom Stella says, there is nothing kinky here, nothing far out, in the music at least. Balconies overlook the sizable dance floor with cozy nooks and booths, perfect for watching the dancing in privacy. There are seats on the main floor for concerts, which are planned for the near future. Behind the balconies is the Champagne Bar, an informal V.I.P. lounge, where card holders and guests of the management enjoy a private club atmosphere. This atmosphere is one the Riviera intends to foster. There is a red pass, good for six months, which you can buy for $100. It admits the holder free and a guest at half price. A gold card is good for a year, costs $300, and admits both holder and guest free. Finally, a platinum card costs $1000 and admits the holder and up to 5 guests to the club and to the Champagne Bar.

In the same spirit, cover prices are fairly high $8 for admissions on Wednesday, Thursday and Saturday nights, $10 on Friday and Saturday nights. On special occasions, like Halloween, covers go up to $15. Drinks start at $2.50; they are very good. There is also a dress code, and you need to be dressed up. If you drive, you might want to use the $4 valet service, because the neighborhood, although improving, is not the greatest. However, Riviera's floodlights and uniformed doormen certainly lend tone to the area. Neiman Marcus held its fall fur show here and Intrinsic paraded its fall models too, amid the lasers and spinning lights. -JJ

SMART BAR / CABARET METRO

3730 N Clark / 60657   549-4140
Hours: Sun–Fri 9:30 pm–4 am, Sat 'til 5 am
CC: Cash Only

The best crossover punk and new wave music anywhere can be heard at this four floor establishment a stone's throw from Wrigley Field. The building was erected in 1927 as a Swedish men's club but now, thanks to owners Joe Shannaker and Joe Prino, it has the right kind of hot and sultry appeal for the mostly young crowd, who arrive decked out in glitter, vintage clothes and torn sweatshirt costumes.

Starting from the bottom: the Smart Bar itself is in the basement. It's dark and gritty, but strangely inviting. The cement floors tend to get rather slippery by the end of the evening, even with the addition of a layer of sawdust. The dance floor is separated from the bar by a chainlink fence and, when I was there, glow-in-the-dark graffiti hung on the walls, part of a constantly changing display of artwork. The very loud music stimulates the crowd—a real melting-pot of people; black, white, Hispanic—to dance up a storm.

The first and second floors make up what is called the Cabaret Metro, which functions as a concert hall and also as a video dance club called Video Metro. On Friday nights groups play American rock music. On Sunday nights an intense group come to hear heavy metal or hard rock groups, some of which are English and German. On Friday and Saturday nights, after concerts, the concert room becomes Video Metro. Tickets for the concerts sell for $10 to $13 and it's worth it, even if this isn't your kind of music, to come at least once and enjoy the contrast between the old rococo setting and the up-to-the-minute crowd.

There are three video screens, 9 by 12 feet, which dominate not only the lower level where the dancing is, but the balcony level as well, where tables are set up. The video has an almost overpowering effect on this enormous, crowded room.

On the top floor is the newest addition to the family, a semi-private club called Joz Place: you need a special card to get in. The cards are issued by the manager, Tom Doody, and what you get is access to a reception bar area, a dance room, a private meeting room and a cozy theatre where you can watch new movies. Joz Place had been decorated by artist Will Northerner who has given the rooms and the long hallway that separates them bright colors and primitive motifs. It's a nice place to get away from the crowded lower floors, to dance, talk or just hang around. Occasionally there are concerts up there too.

The Smart Bar is open Sundays through Thursdays (except for concert nights) and the cover is $2 on Thursdays; no cover the other nights. On Friday and Saturday you can have the run of all three floors for $6: four floors, of course, if you have a Joz Place card, in which case two can get in for the price of one. Drinks cost $1.50 to $2.50. –AT

ZUM LIEBEN AUGUSTIN

4600 N Lincoln / 60625   334-2919

Hours: Tues–Fri 11:30 am–2 am, Sat 11:30 am–3 am, Sun 4 pm–2 am
CC: A, D, M, V

This German restaurant and night club features music and dancing on weekends. Johnny Gruber, the band leader, plays the drums and sings and yodels. The owners are Victor and Lynn Zane. Zane plays in the Germania Combo and even though the Zanes are Rumanian, they offer a German menu. Full course dinners and lunches are inexpensive and so are the drinks. Enjoy a Schnitzel Augustin and an imported German beer from the Zane's large selection; you will have fun dancing to the polka and the waltz on the tiny dance floor. –MC

CESZA LESNA

3356 N Milwaukee / 60641   794-0401
Hours: Fri & Sun 8 pm–3 am, Sat 8 pm–5 am
CC: Cash Only

Despite its nondescript exterior and its gaudy interior with red flocked wallpaper, this Polish club is fun. On Friday and Saturday nights the Polish band Grupa Centrum plays and sings American pop music and show tunes while the neighborhood clientele dances and enjoys itself at the comfortable tables. No cover charge and no minimum. Beer and cocktails are moderately priced and the service is good, although the hostesses are less than secure in English and language difficulties crop up. –MC

HOLIDAY BALLROOM

4847 N Milwaukee / 60630   283-9040
Hours: Fri 7:30 pm–12 am, Sat 6 pm–12:30 am, Sun 6:30 pm–10:30 pm
CC: Cash Only

This is one of the very last of the great dance halls—a relic of another time but very much alive. So, ballroom dancers—and anyone who is ready for an evening of old standards performed by the Freddie Mills band or others like them—break out your dancing shoes and your best vintage bib-and-tucker! It's fun to come here with a group and switch partners. Or just watch the fine ballroom dancers moving under the slowly rotating disco ball. Drinks average $1.50, $1.25 for a bottle of beer. –AT

IRON CURTAIN POLISH JAZZ CLUB

4439 W Fullerton / 60639   878-9766
Hours: Weekends only, 7 pm–2 am
CC: Cash Or Check Only

This storefront club is off the beaten track but well worth the trip. Basha and Pakis Nikokiris have opened it as a gathering place for the growing Polish intellectual community in the city. It is small, and seating is concert style. For the Polish-speaking there are cabaret acts, comedians and plays. If cabaret for non-speakers of Polish is planned, an ad announces that in the *Reader.* Also for English speakers, there are jazz and blues. Adam Mankiewicz, a jazz pianist, comes all the way from New York to perform here. Polish films are shown, some with English sub-titles. Cover charges vary, but they are fairly low. Drinks are cheap and there is no minimum. Reservations are sometimes necessary, so you had better call first.

NOTE: Pakis and Basha have recently opened an art gallery called The Transatlantic which will exhibit work by Polish-American artists every four weeks. Location is 6105 W. Belmont. Call Iron Curtain for information. –MC

MARYLA NIGHT CLUB POLONAISE

3196 N Milwaukee / 60618   545-4152
Entertainment: Fri & Sun 8 pm–4 am, Sat 'til 5 am
Bar: 10 am–4 am
CC: Cash Only

You can spend your entire evening dining on excellent Polish or American food here and dancing to the music of various eastern European bands. There is a cover charge of $3 whether you dine or not, but everything is fairly cheap. Things don't really get going until after midnight; this is a favorite last stop for people visiting Polish clubs in the neighborhood. One group that performs here is the Happy Band, featuring a female singer who belts out Polish and American popular songs. The dance floor is large, but watch out for the apple tree growing in the middle if you're going to do any twirling. –MC

TANIA'S

2659 N Milwaukee / 60647   235-7120
Hours: Daily 11 am–Midnight
Entertainment: Fri–Sun 9:30 pm
CC A, D, M, V

This Cuban night club and restaurant is owned by the Sánchez family. On weekends the music is salsa. You can eat dinner here, or just have a snack between dances. There is no cover charge or minimum. But it is best to dress up; people come here looking elegant. –MC

A TOUCH OF EUROPE

5415 W Irving Park Rd / 60641   545-2224
Hours: Fri, Sat, Sun 9 pm–1:30 am
CC: A, M, V

This club caters to Central and Eastern Europeans; the owner, Marco Loncar, is from Croatia. If loud live music and a distinctly singles environment appeal to you, this is a good place for dancing. Between sets you can choose from a variety of sandwiches and simple dinners if you are hungry. Entertainment is live on weekends only, the rest of the week Marco turns his club over to ethnic and De Paul student neighborhood organizations. This is a popular place to hold benefits and stage special events. Call for information. -MC

CHECKER BOARD LOUNGE

423 E 43rd St / 60653   624-3240
Hours: Sun–Fri Noon–2 am, Sat Noon–3 am
CC: Cash Only

This neighborhood blues bar has a real down-home feeling. Owner Buddy Grey is a musician himself, with an excellent group. Another good group that plays here is the Billie Always Band. So settle in at a long table with the mixed crowd of local people, University of Chicago students and regular customers who have travelled—some of them—long distances to hear their favorite groups, eat popcorn and have a good time. Cover charge is $2 Sunday through Wednesday and $3 Thursday through Saturday. The music starts around 10 pm. –MC

CHICKRICK'S (CHICKRICK HOUSE)

2512 S Michigan Ave / 60616   326-1515
Hours: Sun–Fri 11 am–4 am, Sat 11 am–5 am
CC: Cash or Check Only

This is one of Chicago's largest night clubs, with a show room and a disco. The bar is two-level and its green chairs glow in the dark. The drinks are expensive, and really pack a punch. Happy Hour is very lively because Chickrick's, located near several South Side hospitals and office buildings, is a popular after-work spot. On weekends hundreds of loyal fans pack the place and it really takes off. On Friday and Saturday night, blues and pop bands play to an appreciative crowd. Cover in the show room varies, but there is always a cover in the disco, which is one of the best in town, with good sound and lighting. After midnight the dance floor is very crowded. You can dress casually, but patrons are usually dressed up. When I was there, I saw at least 50 women wearing hand-beaded or sequined hats and dresses. –MC

FANTASY NIGHT CLUB

1638 W 79th St / 60620   994-4797
Hours: Bar Daily, 4 pm–4 am, Disco, 9 pm–4 am,
Sat 9 pm–5 am
CC: A, M, V

This singles bar and disco has comfortable seating and super good cocktails. But if you don't want to drink and sit, this is a really hot place to dance. Cover charge is $5, but drinks are on the expensive side: $4 for cocktails. But there is no minimum so if you are a dancer and not a drinker you can have a nice budget evening here. There are large TV and video screens in both the bar and the disco. When there is live entertainment, the cover charge goes up to $10. Gloria Lynn appears here often and WGCI disc jockeys present frequent hot mix shows. During the week there are fashion shows and other special events. The crowd is generally under forty. Remember the casual dress code before you come: no sloppy jeans, no tennis shoes, and jackets for men are preferred. –MC

MOTHER'S STEAK HOUSE AND LOUNGE

2635 E 79th St / 60649   731-2600
Hours: Bar/Rest 12 pm–4 am
Entertainment: Fri, Sat, Sun, 9 pm–4 am
CC: Cash Only

A great big fancy bar is the second-best feature of this restaurant-lounge. The best feature is the live music played on weekends within a few feet of wherever you might be sitting. Various Chicago blues bands star here: some nights the range of music runs from jazz to crossover to pop—but whatever it is, the evening sparkles. People come dressed any way they like—jeans, spangled dresses—whatever. Drinks: $2 to $3.50. –AT

THE NEW APARTMENT LOUNGE

504 E 75th St / 60619   483-7728
Hours: Daily, Noon–4 am, Sat 'til 5 am
CC: Cash Only

This is a cozy neighborhood club which offers live jazz entertainment in a congenial atmosphere for the over-thirty crowd. The after-work happy hour is popular with merchants and office workers in the area and it is a lovely place to enjoy your after-dinner drink. Arthur Prysock and other entertainers sing in the Red Entertainment Room adjoining the bar. Prysock usually gives 7 or 8 performances here whenever he comes to Chicago. Organist Jimmy McGriff appears once or twice a year, and Von Freeman and his jazz band play every Monday and Tuesday night. Sets are longer and drinks are cheaper here than at most downtown clubs. Call for entertainment schedules. –MC

THE OTHER PLACE

377 E 75th St / 60619   874-5476
Hours: Daily, 1 pm–4 am

Entertainment: Mon, Tues, Wed, Thurs, Fri, 10:30 pm, 12:30 am, 2:30 am; Sat, & Sun 11 pm, 1 am, 3 am
CC: Cash Only

This is a real musicians' jazz bar where even on off nights local musicians jump at the chance to fill in for awhile. The club has two rooms, but the stage can be seen from any place you sit. The walls are covered with photographs of Cab Calloway, Earl Hines, Billy Eckstine, Billie Holliday and many, many others—it is a gallery of the history of Chicago jazz. And there are contemporaries, too, who stop in here—Della Reese, Sarah Vaughan, Joe Williams, Sammy Davis and Lamar Burton.

The night I was there, the Chris Foreman Experience was playing fabulous jazz. They were sharing their chairs off and on with musicians from the Chicago Motivators and King Fleming Trio. Musical choices are left to the evening's band leader and you never know what to expect. It's like being at a jam session.

On weekends the club is crowded and noisy. Although it's less noisy on weeknights, it's never the place for intimate conversation.

Maceo Jones, the proprietor, says his patrons are the parents and grandparents of young people who frequent discos and punk bars. It's a lively well-dressed crowd: neighborhood people stop in before 9 pm, and after that business people and politicians arrive. There's a large photograph of Harold Washington on the stage and near the entrance one of Walter Dyett who taught music at Du Sable High School, when Maceo was there, to some of the most famous jazz musicians in the country.

Maceo bought the club when he retired from the Chicago police force. It is a success because the music is great and the place is comfortable and well run. There is no cover, no minimum, and drinks and snacks are moderately priced. –MC

THERESA'S

607 E 43rd St / 60653   285-2744
Hours: Daily, 9 pm–2 am
CC: Cash Only

Chicago's best, most popular blues bands play here seven nights a week. Monday is jam session night, with free spaghetti. On weekends the large room fills with an interesting diversity of patrons. The decor and lighting leave a lot to be desired, but the entertainment is first rate. –MC

BABY DOLL POLKA CLUB

6102 S Central/60638   582-9706
Hours: Mon–Fri 5 pm–2 am, Sat 9:30 pm–3 am, Sun 9:30 pm–2 am
Entertainment: Fri & Sat 9:30 pm–3 am Sun 5 pm–Midnight
CC: Cash Only

For more than 30 years this has been the premier polka stomping ground. Eddie and Irene Korosa are the owners: he is known as the Prince of Polka and she is vivacious and friendly. The hordes of regulars who whoop it up night after night offer proof positive that the Baby Doll deserves its reputation as one of the liveliest bars in town. The wonderfully garish '50s carpet holds up amazingly under the wear and tear as customers make their way to the impossibly small dance floor, return to their seats and then, unable to resist the intoxicating music, wend their way back to dance once more. This continues until the band breaks and the crowd takes over. The night we were there, an enthusiastic female customer led the room in renditions of old favorites—including the most spirited "God Bless America" that I had sung since the third grade.

Obviously no one is afraid to have a good time here. Eddie Korosa and the Merrymakers have been around, as they say, forever. Eddie is not only one of the world's best button box accordianists, but he wrote "The Baby Doll Polka" and other polka standards. He and the Merrymakers have made dozens of records and for years he and Irene were the hosts of their own TV and radio shows, the latter emanating from the Baby Doll itself.

Irene mingles with the customers, welcoming each arrival herself. Her list of friends must be longer than the Merrymakers' version of "She's Too Fat For Me." There is no cover; drinks run from $1.25 to $2. So drop in at The Baby Doll and become part of the polka scene. –AT

AKA, 6259 N. Broadway, (274-6657)
Video dance club

Acorn on Oak, 116 E. Oak, (944-6835), *Piano bar*

The Ali Baba, 8530 S. Pulaski, (767-1118), *Arab*

Antibes, 1824 Augusta Blvd., (486-1400)
Jazz and ethnic

Aquarius Inn, 201 W. Madison, (322-1116), *Jazz*

Arnies, 1030 N. State, (266-4800), *Piano bar*

Ash Manor, 1600 W. Diversey, (248-1600),
Piano bar

Aziza, 6239 S. Kedzie, (471-1120),
Arabic belly dancers

Backroom, 1007 N. Rush, (751-2443), *Jazz*

Baton Lounge, 436 N. Clark, (644-5269),
Female impersonators

Benny's Lounge, 2201 W. Montrose, (463-0044),
Arab

Billy's, 936 N. Rush, (943-7080), *Jazz*

Buffoons, 1934 W. Irving Park, (871-3757),
Rock bands on Saturday nights

By Chance, 714 E. 79th St., (846-0728), *Jazz*

Byfield's, 1301 N. State Parkway, (787-6433),
Eclectic cabaret

Caribbean Village, 1706 E. 75th St., (363-3065),
Reggae, calypso, and West Indian music, dancing

Celebration Lounge, 7301 W. Forest Preserve, (625-3221), *Pop and jazz*

Club Victoria, 3153 N. Broadway, (528-7988), *Eclectic cabaret, female impersonators*

Connelly's, 8434 S. Kedzie, (476-3646), *Blues and rock*

Crystal Palace Show Club, 11935 S. Michigan, (264-4384), *Blues*

Cubby Bear Lounge, 1059 W. Addison, (327-1662), *Reggae, Rock bands after Cubs games, dancing*

Cuddle Inn Lounge, 5317 S. Ashland, (778-1999), *Blues*

The Dairy, 1936 W. Augusta Blvd., (252-4090), *Restaurant with live entertainment on weekends*

Dandy's, 2632 N. Halsted, (975-6373), *Rock*

Der Read Barron, 2265 N. Lincoln, (848-8730), *Comedy revue and improvisation*

Desanka's Place, 4343 N. Lincoln, (525-8171), *Yugoslavian*

Duke of Alba at Toldeo, 1935 N. Sedgewick, (266-2066), *Spanish*

Earl of Old Town, 1615 N. Wells, (642-5206), *Folk*

Fifth Wheel Lounge, 4443 S. Halsted, (536-9497), *Country*

Gaspar's, 3159 N. Southport, (871-6680), *Occasional comedy revues and improvisation*

The Ginger Man, 3740 N. Clark, (549-2050), *Occasional comedy revues and improvisation*

The Greenmill Cocktail Lounge, 4802 N. Broadway, (878-5552), *Show tunes, golden oldies, blues on Sunday nights*

Holstein's, 2464, (327-3331), *Folk*

Hummingbird Supper Club, 8620 S. Ashland Ave., (445-0500), *Reggae*

Hunt Club, 1938 N. Clybourn, (549-3020), *Restaurant with jazz combos*

Improvisation Institute, 2939 W. Belmont, (588-2668), *Comedy revue and improvisation*

Irish Village, 6215 W. Diversey, (237-7555), *Irish*

Iron Rail Pub, 5843 W. Irving Park, (736-4670), *Rock*

Keefe's, 3714 N. Clark, (472-4843), *Occasional comedy revue and improvisation*

Keenan O'Malley's, 2125 W. Roscoe, (348-8712), *Rock and folk*

Kiku's, 754 Wellington, (281-7878), *Jazz*

Kilkenny Castle Inn, 3808 N. Central, (736-0709), *Irish*

Kingston Mines, 2548 N. Halsted, (477-4646), *Blues*

Lakeview Lounge, 5110 N. Broadway, (769-0994), *Country*

Lee's Unleaded Blues, 7401 S. Chicago, (493-3477), *Blues*

Lilly's, 2515 N. Lincoln Ave., (525-2422), *Blues*

Lion Bar, Westin Hotel, 909 N. Michigan, (943-7200), *Jazz*

Living Room, 744 E. 83rd St., (846-4160), *Blues*

Lonnie's Skyway Lounge, 135 W. 75th St., (488-6522), *Jazz and rhythm and blues*

Medusa, Sheffield & School Sts., (935-3635/549-9272), *New wave*

Milt Trenier's Lounge, 600 N. Lake Shore Dr., (266-6226), *Jazz and pop*

Miomir's, 2255 W. Lawrence, (784-2111), *Serbian restaurant with musical entertainment*

Moose's Lounge, 4553 N. Pulaski, (539-0410), *Country*

Moscow at Night, 3058 W. Peterson, (338-6600), *Russian and continental*

Mr. Lump's Showcase, 3842 W. Madison, (265-6535), *Blues, jazz, pop*

Negril, 6232 N. Broadway, (761-4133), *Reggae, dancing*

Orphans, 2462 N. Lincoln, (929-2677), *Swing, salsa, and jazz, dancing*

O'Sullivan's Public House, 495 N. Milwaukee Ave., (733-2927), *Blues, rock, and big band jazz*

The Rafters, 9757 S. Commercial, (731-0288),
  Yugoslavian

Rick's Cafe American, 644 N. Lake Shore Dr.,
  Nationally known jazz entertainers

Rosa's Lounge, 3420 W. Armitage, (342-0452),
  Blues

Sahara, 3304 W. Fullerton, (772-6964),
  Arabic belly dancers

Second City, 1616 N. Wells, (337-3992),
  Comedy revue and improvisation

Second City Etc., 1608 N. Wells, (642-8189),
  Comedy revue and improvisation

Sevon, 6351 N. Claremont, (465-0080),
  Middle Eastern/Bellydancing

Skorpios, 2811 N. Central, (736-8488), *Greek*

Tania's on the Lake, 400 E. Randolph, (861-0225),
  Jazz and folk

The Theater Building, 1225 W. Belmont,
  (327-5252), *Dramatic theater
  which occasionally features comedy improvisation.*

Tony's, 2824 W. Fullerton, (342-8080), *Latin*

U.S. Blues, 1446 N. Wells, (266-4978), *Blues*

ENTERTAINMENT GUIDE

See pages 207-208 for page numbers

Club names followed by a "P" will be found under POTPOURRI at the end of the main section of the book.

ARAB MUSIC

The Ali Baba
Benny's Lounge

BLUES CLUBS

Biddy Mulligan's
Blue Chicago
B.L.U.E.S.
Checkerboard Lounge
Chickrick's
Connolly's (P)
Crystal Palace
  Show Club (P)
Cuddle Inn Lounge (P)
Kingston Mines (P)
Lee's Unleaded Blues
  (P)
Lilly's (P)
Living Room (P)
Mr. Lump's Showcase
  (P)
Mother's Steak House
  & Lounge (Thurs) (P)
Orphan's (P)

O'Sullivan's
  Public House (P)
Rick's American Cafe (P)
Tania's On The Lake
  (P)
Theresa's (P)
Trampps (P)
U.S. Blues (P)

CHAMPAGNE BARS

Pops for Champagne
Riviera

COFFEE HOUSES

No Exit Cafe

COMEDY

Chicago
  Comedy Showcase
Cross Currents
Der Read Barron (P)
Gaspar's (P)
  Occasional comedy
  review & improv.

COMEDY Continued

Ginger Man (P)
  Occasional comedy
  review & improv.
Improvisation Institute
  (P)
Keefe's (P)
  Occasional comedy
  review & improv.
Opal Station
The Roxy
Second City (P)
Second City Etc. (P)
Theater Building (P)
  Occasional comedy
  review & improv.

COUNTRY

Fifth Wheel Lounge (P)
Lakeview Lounge (P)
Moose's Lounge (P)

DANCING

AKA (P)
Artful Dodger
Asi es Colombia
Baby Doll Polka Club
Berlin
Biddy Mulligan's

Blue Chicago
Cafe Continental
Caribbean Village (P)
Cesza Lesna
Chickrick's
Coconuts
Cubby Bear Lounge (P)
Exit
Fantasy Night Club
Holiday Ballroom
The Latin Village
The Limelight
Maryla Night
  Club Polonaise
Medusa (P)
Negril (P)
Neo
The Octagon Pub
Orphans (P)
Paradise
Park West Video
  Dance Party
The Rainbo Club
Riviera
Smart Bar/
  Cabaret Metro
Tania's
A Touch of Europe
The Vic Theater
The Vu Bar & Grill
West End

DANCING
Continued

The Wild Hare
  & Singing Armadillo
  Frog Sanctuary
Zum Lieben Augustin

ECLECTIC MUSIC

Artful Dodger
The Bulls
Byfield's (P)
Coconuts
Cross Currents
Dixie Bar & Grill
Get Me High Lounge
Limelight
Mother's Steak House
  & Lounge
Neo
The 950 Club-
  "Lucky Number"
The Octagon Pub
O'Sullivan's
  Public House
Opal Station
Paradise
The Raccoon Club
The Rainbo Club
The Roxy
The Vic Theatre

FOLK

Earl of Old Town (P)
Holstein's (P)
Keenan O'Malley's (P)
No Exit Cafe
Tania's On the Lake (P)
  (also jazz)

GERMAN

Zum Lieben Augustin

GREEK

Deni's Den Restaurant
  & Club
Skorpios (P)

IRISH

Irish Village
Kilkenny Castle Inn

JAZZ

Andy's
Aquarius Inn (P)
Backroom (P)
Billy's (P)
By Chance (P)
Celebration Lounge (P)
Cross Currents

JAZZ Continued

George's
Hunt Club (P)
Iron Curtain Polish
   Jazz Club
Joe Segal's
   Jazz Showcase
Kiku's (P)
Lion Bar (P)
Lonnie's Skyway
   Lounge (P) (and
   rhythm & blues)
Milt Trenier's Lounge
   (P) (and pop)
Moosehead Bar & Grill
New Apartment Lounge
The Other Place
Oz
Paradise
Pops for Champagne
The Raccoon Club
Tania's On The Lake
   (P) (with folk)
The Vu Bar & Grill
Yvette

Tania's
Tony's (P)

CENTRAL
& EASTERN EUROPEAN

Baby Doll Polka Club
   (Polish)
Cafe Continental
Cesza Lesna (Polish)
Desanka's Place
   (Yugoslavian)
Iron Curtain
   Polish Jazz Club
Maryla Night
   Club Polonaise
Miomir's (P)
   (Serbian)
Moscow at Night
   (P) (Russian)
The Rafters (P)
   (Yugoslavian)
Sevon (P)
A Touch of Europe

LATIN CLUBS

Asi es Colombia
The Latin Village

NOSTALGIA:
VINTAGE MUSIC

Dixie Bar & Grill
   (some nights)

The Green Mill
Cocktail Lounge (P)
Holiday Ballroom
Jukebox Saturday Night
Raccoon Club
(some nights)

PIANO BARS

Acorn on Oak (P)
Arnie's (P)
Ash Manor (P)
Beverly Hills Cafe
Rendezvous
Trampps (P)

POP

Cafe Continental
Celebration Lounge (P)
Cesza Lesna
Chickrick's
Fantasy Night Club
Jukebox Saturday Night
Milt Trenier's Lounge

PUNK & NEW WAVE

Exit
Neo
950 Club-
"Lucky Number"
Octagon Pub

Smart Bar/
Cabaret Metro
West End

REGGAE

Biddy Mulligan's
Cubby Bear Lounge (P)
Hummingbird
Supper Club (P)
Negril (P)
Wild Hare
& Singing Armadillo
Frog Sanctuary

SPANISH

The Duke of Alba
at Toledo (P)

VIDEO CLUBS

AKA (P)
Berlin
Cabaret Metro
Exit
Fantasy Night Club
Neo
The 950 Club-
"Lucky Number"
Park West Video
Dance Party

ALPHABETICAL INDEX TO CLUBS
(See Also Potpourri Section)

A

Andy's	145
Artful Dodger	155
Asi Es Colombia	173

B

Baby Doll Polka Club	195
Berlin	155
Beverly Hills Cafe	141
Biddy Mulligan's	173
Blue Chicago	146
B.L.U.E.S.	156
The Bulls	156

C

Cafe Continental	174
Cesza Lesna	185
Checkerboard Lounge	189
Chicago Comedy Showcase	176
Chickrick's (Chickrick House)	189
Coconuts	177
Cross Currents	157

D

Deni's Den Restaurant & Lounge	157
Dixie Bar and Grill	147

E

Exit	148

F

Fantasy Night Club	190

G

George's	148
Get Me High Lounge	150

H

Holiday Ballroom	185

I

Iron Curtain Polish Jazz Club	186

J

Joe Segal's Jazz Showcase	141
Jukebox Saturday Night	159

L

The Latin Village	160
Limelight	150

M

Maryla Night Club Polonaise	186
Medusa's	160
Moosehead Bar & Grill	142
Mother's Steak House & Lounge	190

N

Neo	161
New Apartment Lounge	191
The 950 Club	162
No Exit	178

O

The Octagon Pub	163
Opal Station	179
The Other Place	191
Oz	163

P

Paradise	164
Park West Video Dance Party	165
Pops for Champagne	165

R

The Raccoon Club	151
The Rainbo Club	166
Rendezvous	152
Riviera	180
The Roxy	167

S

Smart Bar/ Cabaret Metro	182

T

Tania's	187
Theresa's	193
A Touch of Europe	187

V

The Vic Theatre	168
The Vu Bar and Grill	170

W

West End	171
The Wild Hare & Singing Armadillo Frog Sanctuary	171

Y

Yvette	153

Z

Zanie's Comedy Club	153
Zum Lieben Augustin	183